The Liberal Virus

The Liberal Virus

Permanent War and the Americanization of the World

Samir Amin

Translated by James H. Membrez

First published 2004 by Pluto Press
New Wing, Somerset House, Strand, London WC2R 1LA

www.plutobooks.com

British Library Cataloguing in Publication Data
A catalogue record for this book is available from the British Library

ISBN 978 0 7453 2359 6   Paperback

Typeset by Riverside Publishing Solutions
Printed and bound by CPI Group (UK) Ltd, Croydon, CR0 4YY

Contents

Introduction

Towards The End Of The Twentieth Century a sickness
struck the world. Not everyone died, but all suffered from
it. The virus which caused the epidemic was called the
"liberal virus". This virus made its appearance around
the sixteenth century within the triangle described by
Paris–London–Amsterdam. The symptoms that the
disease then manifested appeared harmless. Men (whom
the virus struck in preference to women) not only became
accustomed to it and developed the necessary antibodies,
but were able to benefit from the increased energy that it
elicited. But the virus traveled across the Atlantic and
found a favorable place among those who, deprived of
antibodies, spread it. As a result, the malady took on
extreme forms.

The virus reappeared in Europe towards the end of
the twentieth century, returning from America where it
had mutated. Now strengthened, it came to destroy a
great number of the antibodies that the Europeans had
developed over the course of the three preceding
centuries. It provoked an epidemic that would have been
fatal to the human race if it had not been for the most
robust of the inhabitants of the old countries who
survived the epidemic and finally were able to eradicate
the disease.

The virus caused among its victims a curious

schizophrenia. Humans no longer lived as whole beings, organizing themselves to produce what is necessary to satisfy their needs (what the learned have called "economic life") and simultaneously developing the institutions, the rules, and the customs that enable them to develop (what the same learned people have called "political life"), conscious that the two aspects of social life are inseparable. Henceforth, they lived sometimes as *homo oeconomicus*, abandoning to "the market" the responsibility to regulate their "economic life" automatically, and sometimes as "citizens", depositing in ballot boxes their choices for those who would have the responsibility to establish the rules of the game for their "political life".

The crises of the end of the twentieth century and the beginning of the twenty-first century, now happily and definitively left behind, were articulated around the confusions and impasses provoked by this schizophrenia. Reason—the true one, not the American one—finally caused it to disappear. Everyone survived, Europeans, Asians, Africans, Americans, and even Texans, who have much changed since and become human beings like the others.

I have chosen this happy ending, not through some incorrigible optimism, but because in the other hypothesis there would no longer be anyone left to write history. In that version, Fukuyama was right: liberalism truly announced the end of history. All of humanity perished in the holocaust. The last survivors, the Texans, were organized into a wandering band and then immolated in turn, on the orders of the chief of their sect, whom they had believed to be a charismatic figure. He too was named Bush.

I imagine that the history of our epoch will be

written somewhat in these terms. In any case, it is in the same terms that I here propose to analyze these crises.

I. The "Liberal" Vision of Society

The General Ideas which govern the dominant liberal vision of the world are simple and may be summarized in the following terms :

Social effectiveness is equated by liberals with economic efficiency which, in turn, is confounded with the financial profitability of capital. These reductions express the dominance of the economic, a dominance characteristic of capitalism. The atrophied social thought derived from this dominance is "economistic" in the extreme. Curiously, this reproach, wrongly directed at Marxism, in fact characterizes capitalist liberalism.

The development of the generalized market (the least regulated possible) and of democracy are decreed to be complementary to one another. The question of conflict between social interests which are expressed through their interventions in the market and social interests which give meaning and import to political democracy is not even posed. Economics and politics do not form two dimensions of social reality, each having their own autonomy, operating in a dialectical relationship; capitalist economics in fact governs the political, whose creative potential it eliminates.

Apparently, the most "developed" country, the one in which the political is actually conceived and practiced entirely in the exclusive service of the economy (of capital, in fact)—obviously the United States—is held to be the best model for "all". Its institutions and practices should be imitated by all those who hope to be contemporary with the world scene.

There is no alternative to the proposed model, which is founded on economistic postulates, the identity of the market and democracy, and the subsumption of the political by the economic. The socialist option attempted in the Soviet Union and China demonstrated that it was both inefficient in economic terms and antidemocratic in the political sphere.

In other words, the propositions formulated above have the virtue of being "eternal truths" (the truths of "Reason") revealed by the unfolding of contemporary history. Their triumph is assured, particularly since the disappearance of the alternative "socialist" experiments. We will all truly arrive, as has been said, at the end of history. Historical Reason has triumphed. This triumph means then that we live in the best of all possible worlds, at least potentially, in the sense that it will be so when its founding ideas are accepted by everyone and put into practice everywhere. All the defects of today's reality are due only to the fact that these eternal principles of Reason are not yet put into practice in the societies that suffer from these deficiencies, particularly those in the global South.

The hegemonism of the United States, a normal expression of its avant-garde position in using Reason (inevitably liberal), is thus both unavoidable and favorable to the progress of the whole of humanity. There is no "American imperialism", only a noble leadership ("benign" or painless, as liberal American intellectuals qualify it).

These "ideas" are central to the liberal vision. In

fact, as we will see in what follows, these ideas are nothing but nonsense, founded on a para-science—so-called pure economics—and an accompanying ideology—postmodernism.

"Pure" economics is not a theory of the real world, of really-existing capitalism, but of an imaginary capitalism. It is not even a rigorous theory of the latter. The bases and development of the arguments do not deserve to be qualified as coherent. It is only a para-science, closer in fact to sorcery than to the natural sciences which it pretends to imitate. As for postmodernism, it only forms an accompanying discourse, calling upon us to act only within the limits of the liberal system, to "adjust" to it.

The reconstruction of a citizen politics demands that movements of resistance, protest and struggle against the real effects of the implementation of this system be freed from the liberal virus.

II. The Ideological and Para-Theoretical Foundations of Liberalism

1. IMAGINARY CAPITALISM AND THE PARA-THEORY OF "PURE" ECONOMICS

The Concept of Capitalism cannot be reduced to the "generalized market", but instead situates the essence of capitalism precisely in power beyond the market. This reduction, as found in the dominant vulgate, substitutes the theory of an imaginary system governed by "economic laws" (the "market") which would tend, if left to themselves, to produce an "optimal equilibrium", for the analysis of capitalism based on social relations and a politics through which these powers beyond the market are expressed. In really-existing capitalism, class struggle, politics, the state, and the logics of capital accumulation are inseparable. Consequently, capitalism is by nature a regime in which the successive states of disequilibrium are products of social and political confrontations situated beyond the market. The concepts proposed by the vulgar economics of liberalism—such as "deregulation" of the markets—have no reality. So-called deregulated markets are markets regulated by the forces of monopolies which are situated outside the market.

Economic alienation[1] is the specific form of capitalism which governs the reproduction of society in its totality and not only the reproduction of its economic system. The law of value governs not only capitalist economic life, but all social life in this society. This specificity explains why, in capitalism, the economic is erected into a "science"—that is, the laws which govern the movement of capitalism are imposed on modern societies (and on the human beings which form those societies) "like laws of nature". In other words, the fact that these laws are the product not of a transhistorical nature (which would define the "human being" vis-à-vis the challenge of "scarcity") but of a particular historical nature (social relations specifically characteristic of capitalism) is erased from social consciousness. This is, in my opinion, how Marx understood "economism", the unique characteristic of capitalism.

In addition, Marx brings to light the immanent instability of this society, in the sense that the reproduction of its economic system never tends towards the realization of any sort of general equilibrium, but is displaced from disequilibrium to disequilibrium in an unforeseeable manner. One can account for this after the fact but never define it in advance. The "competition" between capitals—which defines capitalism—suppresses the possibility of realizing any sort of general equilibrium and thus renders illusory any analysis founded on such a supposed tendency. Capitalism is synonymous with permanent instability. The articulation between the logics produced by this competition of capitals and those which are deployed through the evolution of the social relations of production (among capitalists, between them and the exploited and dominated classes, among the states which form capitalism as a world system) accounts, after the fact, for the movement of the system as it displaces itself from one disequilibrium to another. In this sense, capitalism does not exist outside of the class struggle, the conflict between states, and politics. The idea that there exists an economic logic '(which economic science enables us to discover) that governs the development of capitalism is an illusion. There is no theory of capitalism distinct from its history. Theory and history are indissociable, just as are economics and politics.

I have pointed out these two dimensions of Marx's radical critique precisely because these are the two dimensions of reality of which bourgeois social thought is ignorant. This thought is, in fact, economistic from its origins in the era of the Enlightenment. The "Reason" that it invokes attributes to the capitalist system, which replaces the Ancien Regime, a transhistorical legitimacy making it the "end of history". This economic alienation was to be accentuated thereafter, precisely in the attempt to respond to Marx. Pure economics, starting with Walras, expresses this exacerbation of the economism of bourgeois social thought. It substitutes the myth of a self-regulating market, which would tend through its own internal logic towards the realization of a general equilibrium, for the analysis of the real functioning of capitalism. Instability is no longer conceived as immanent to this logic, but as the product of the imperfections of real markets. Economics thus becomes a discourse which is no longer engaged in knowing reality; its function is no more than to legitimize capitalism by attributing to it intrinsic qualities'which it cannot have. Pure economics becomes the theory of an imaginary world.

The dominant forces are such because they succeed in imposing their language on their victims. The "experts" of conventional economics have managed to make believe that their analyses and the conclusions drawn from them are imperative because they are "scientific", hence objective, neutral and unavoidable. This is not true. The so-called pure economics on which they base their analyses does not deal with reality, but with an imaginary system which not only does not approach reality but is located squarely in the opposite direction. Really-existing capitalism is another thing entirely.

This imaginary economics mixes up concepts and confuses progress with capitalist expansion, market with capitalism. In order to develop effective strategies, social movements must liberate themselves from these confusions.

The confusion of two concepts—the reality (capitalist expansion) and the desirable (progress in a determined sense)—is at the origin of many disappointments expressed in the criticisms of implemented policies. The dominant discourses systematically mix up concepts. They propose means that enable the expansion of capital and then qualify as "development" that which results, or would result, according to them. The logic of the expansion of capital does not imply any result qualifiable in terms of "development". It does not suppose, for example, full employment or an amount designated in advance for the unequal (or equal) distribution of income. The logic of this expansion is guided by the search for profits by individual enterprises. This logic can entail, in certain conditions, growth or stagnation, expansion of employment or its reduction, can reduce inequality in incomes or accentuate it, according to circumstances.

Here gain the sustained confusion between the concept of "market economy" and that of "capitalist economy" is at the source of a dangerous weakness found in critiques of the policies that are carried out. The "market", which refers by nature to competition, is not "capitalism", which is defined precisely by the limits to competition that the monopoly or oligopoly (for some people, to the exclusion of others) of private property implies. The "market" and capitalism form two distinct concepts. Really-existing capitalism is, as Braudel's analysis has shown so well, the opposite even of the imaginary market.

In addition, really-existing capitalism does not function as a system of competition among the beneficiaries of the monopoly of property—competition among them and against others. Its operation requires the intervention of a collective authority representing capital as a whole. Thus the state is not separable from capitalism. The policies of capital, thus of the state insofar as it represents capital, have their own concrete logical stages. It is these logical stages that account for the fact that, at certain times, the expansion of capital entails an increase in employment, at other times a decrease in employment. These logical stages are not the expression of "laws of the market", formulated in the abstract as such, but requirements of the profitability of capital in certain historical conditions.

There is no "law of capitalist expansion" which is imposed as a quasi-supernatural force. There is no historical determinism anterior to history. The inherent tendencies of the logic of capital always clash with forces which resist its effects. Real history is thus the product of this conflict between the logic of capitalist expansion and those logics that spring from social forces resisting its expansion. In this sense, the state is rarely simply the state of capital, it is also at the heart of the conflict between capital and society.

For example, the industrialization of the postwar period, from 1945 to 1990, was not the natural product of capitalist expansion but rather resulted from conditions imposed on capital by the victories of national liberation movements, which forced globalizing capital to adjust to this industrialization. For example, the erosion of the effectiveness of the national state, produced by capitalist globalization, is not an irreversible determinant of the future. On the contrary, national reactions to this globalization could impose unforeseen trajectories onto global expansion, for better or worse according to circumstances. For example, the concerns stemming from the environment, which are in conflict with the logic of capital (which is by nature a short-term logic) could impose important transformations onto capitalist adjustment. One could multiply the examples.

The effective response to the challenges can only be found if one understands that history is not governed by the infallible unfolding of economic laws. It is produced by social reactions to the tendencies expressed by these laws which, in turn, are defined by the social relations within the framework in which these laws operate. The "anti-systemic" forces—if one wants to refer to this organized, coherent and effective refusal to the unilateral and total submission to the requirements of these alleged laws (in fact, quite simply the law of profit characteristic of capitalism as a system)—make real history as much as the "pure" logic of capitalist accumulation. These forces govern the possibilities and the forms of the expansion which then develop within the framework that they have organized.

The method proposed here prohibits formulating "recipes" in advance that would allow the future to be made. The future is produced by the transformations in the social and political relations of force, themselves produced by struggles whose outcomes are not known in advance. One can nevertheless reflect on this process, in the context of contributing to the crystallization of coherent and possible projects and, consequently, help any social movement avoid false solutions. In the absence of such reflection, a movement could easily become bogged down in the pursuit of these "solutions".

The project of a humanist response to the challenge of capitalism's globalized expansion is by no means utopian. On the contrary, it is the only possible realistic project, in the sense that the beginning of an evolution towards such a response could rapidly win over powerful social forces capable of imposing a logic on it. If there is a utopia, in the banal and negative sense of the term, it is truly the project of managing the system, understood as regulation by the market.

2. POSTMODERNISM, IDEOLOGICAL ACCESSORY TO LIBERALISM

Postmodernist discourse is an ideological accessory that, in the end, legitimizes liberalism and invites us to submit to it.

The apparent triumph of liberalism—in its most simplistic and brutal North American form—does not express an impulse towards the rejuvenation of capitalism, restoring to it all the American vigor eroded by statism and the welfare state of old Europe. The opposition of "young America"—which has the future before it—to "old Europe" constitutes, as is well known, one of the favored themes of "pro-American" discourse.

The offensive of liberalism strives, in fact, to overcome, through brutality, the growing contradictions of capitalism, which has had its day and has no perspective to offer humanity other than that of self-destruction.

This obsolescence of capitalism is not expressed exclusively in the spheres of economic and social reproduction. Onto this decisive infrastructural base are grafted multiple manifestations both of the retreat of bourgeois universalist thought (for which new ideological discourses substitute a so-called postmodernist patchwork) and of regression in the practices of political management (calling into question the bourgeois democratic tradition).

The ideological discourse of postmodernism is sustained by these regressions. Recuperating every common prejudice produced by the disarray characteristic of moments such as ours, it methodically lays out, without concern for overall coherence, one argument after another encouraging suspicion towards the concepts of progress and universalism. But far from deepening the serious critique of these expressions of Enlightenment culture and bourgeois history, far from analyzing their actual contradictions, which are aggravated by the obsolescence of the system, this discourse is satisfied with substituting the impoverished propositions of liberal American ideology for a true critique : "live with your time", "adapt to it", "manage each day"—that is, abstain from reflecting on the nature of the system, and particularly from calling into question its choices of the moment.

The praise for inherited diversities proposed in place of the necessary effort to transcend the limits of bourgeois universalism thus functions in perfect accord with the requirements of contemporary imperialism's project of globalization, a project that can produce only an organized system of apartheid on a world scale, sustained as it is by reactionary "communitarian" ideologies in the North American tradition. What I qualify as the "culturalist" retreat, which is at the forefront of the scene today, is thus implemented and manipulated by the masters of the system, just as it is equally often seized upon by the dominated peoples in confusion (under the form of so-called religious or ethnic fundamentalisms). This is the "clash of barbarisms", as Gilbert Achcar has written, giving Huntington's thesis a self-realizing character.

The totality of these manifestations of both confusion and retreat in relation to the past achievements of bourgeois thought results in a degradation of political practice. The very principle of democracy is founded on the possibility of making alternative choices. There is no longer a need for democracy, since ideology made the idea that "there is no alternative" acceptable. Adherence to a meta-social principle of superior rationality allows for the elimination of the necessity and possibility of choosing. The so-called principle of the rationality of "markets" exactly fills this function in the ideology of obsolescent capitalism. Democratic practice is thus emptied of all content and the way is open to what I have called "low-intensity democracy"—that is, to electoral buffooneries where parades of majorettes take the place of programs, to the "society of the spectacle". Delegitimized by these practices, politics is undone, begins to drift and loses its potential power to give meaning and coherence to alternative societal projects.

Is not the bourgeoisie itself, as the structured

dominant class, on the way to "changing its look"? All during the ascendant phase of its history, the bourgeoisie was formed as the principal determinant of "civil society". That did not imply a relative stability of men (only a few women in that era) or at least of family dynasties of capitalist-entrepreneurs (competition always implying a certain mobility in the membership of this class, bankruptcies occurring in conjunction with the rise of nouveaux riches) so much as the strong structuring of the class around systems of values and behaviors. The dominant class could then assert that the respectability of its members established the legitimacy of its privileges. This is less and less the case. A model close to that of the mafia seems to be the one taking over in the business world as much as in politics. Moreover, the separation between these two worlds—which, though it was not watertight, nevertheless characterized the systems that preceded historical capitalism—is in the process of disappearing. This model is not characteristic only of Third World countries or of the former so-called socialist countries of the East: it is tending to become the rule even at the heart of central capitalism. How else to characterize persons like Berlusconi in Italy, Bush (implicated in the Enron scandal) in the United States, and many others elsewhere?

But a senile system is not one that shuffles peacefully through its last days. On the contrary, senility summons an increase in violence.

The world system has not entered into a new "non-imperialist" phase that is sometimes characterized as "post-imperialist". On the contrary, it is by nature an imperialist system exacerbated to the extreme (extracting resources without effective opposition). The analysis that Negri and Hardt propose of an "Empire" (without imperialism), in fact an Empire limited to the Triad— that is, the three major regions of capitalism, the United States, Europe, and Japan—with the rest of the world being ignored, is unfortunately inscribed both in the tradition of Occidentalism and in the currently fashionable intellectual discourse. The differences between the new imperialism and the preceding one are found elsewhere. Imperialism in the past was multiple ("imperialisms" in conflict), while the new one is collective (the Triad, even if this be in the wake of United States hegemony). From this fact, the "conflicts" among the partners of the Triad are only minor, while the conflict between the Triad and the rest of the world is clearly the major one. The disappearance of the European project in the face of American hegemonism finds its explanation here. Furthermore, accumulation in the prior imperialist stage was based on the binary relation between the industrialized centers and the non-industrialized peripheries, while in the new conditions of the system's evolution the opposition is between the beneficiaries of the centers' new monopolies (technology, access to natural resources, communications, weapons of mass destruction) and peripheries that are industrialized, but still subordinated by means of these monopolies. In order to justify their thesis, Negri and Hardt need to give a strictly political definition of the imperialist phenomenon ("the projection of national power beyond its frontiers"), without any relation to the requirements for the accumulation and reproduction of capital. This definition, which stems from vulgar university political science, particularly of the North American variety, eliminates from the start the true questions. Their discourse deals with a category "empire" placed outside of history and thus happily makes no distinction among the Roman, Ottoman, Austro-Hungarian, Russian, British colonial, and French colonial empires. No care is taken to consider the specificities of these historical constructions without reducing them to one another.

In fact, the global expansion of capitalism, because it is polarizing, always implies the political intervention of the dominant powers, that is, the states of the system's center, in the societies of the dominated periphery. This expansion cannot occur by the force of economic laws alone; it is necessary to complement that with political support (and military, if necessary) from states in the service of dominant capital. In this sense, the expansion is always entirely imperialist even in the meaning that Negri gives to the term ("the projection of national power beyond its frontiers", on condition of specifying that this power belongs to capital). In this sense, the contemporary intervention of the United States is no less imperialist than were the colonial conquests of the nineteenth century. Washington's objective in Iraq, for example, (and tomorrow elsewhere) is to put in place a dictatorship in the service of American capital (and not a "democracy"), enabling the pillage of the country's natural resources, and nothing more. The globalized "liberal" economic order requires permanent war—military interventions endlessly succeeding one another—as the only means to submit the peoples of the periphery to its demands.

The new-style Empire, on the contrary, is defined naively as a "network of powers" whose center is everywhere and nowhere, which thus dilutes the importance of the national state. This transformation moreover is essentially attributed to the development of the productive forces (the technological revolution). This is a shallow and simplistic analysis that isolates the power of technology from the framework of social relations within which it operates. Once again we recognize here the propositions of the dominant discourse vulgarized by Rawls, Castells, Touraine, Rifkin and others, in the tradition of North American liberal political thought.

The true questions that are posed by the articulation between the political instance (the state) and the reality of globalization, which should be at the center of the analysis of what is possibly "new" in the evolution of the capitalist system, are thus simply evaded by the gratuitous affirmation that the state has almost ceased to exist. In fact, even in the prior stages of an always globalized capitalism, the state was never omnipotent. Its power was always limited by the logic which governed the globalizations of the epoch. Wallerstein has even, in this spirit, gone so far as to give the global determinations a decisive power over the destiny of the states. The situation is no difference today, since the difference between the globalization (imperialism) of the present and that of the past is found elsewhere.

The new imperialism truly has a center—the Triad— and a center of the center aspiring to exercise its hegemony—the United States. The Triad exercises its collective domination over the whole of the planet's peripheries (three-quarters of humanity) by means of institutions put into place and under its management for that purpose. Some institutions are in charge of the economic management of the world imperialist system. Foremost among these are the World Tade Organization (WTO) whose real function is not to guarantee "freedom of markets" as it pretends but, on the contrary, to super-protect the monopolies (of the center) and to form systems of production for the peripheries as a function of this requirement; the IMF, which does not trouble itself with the relationships among the three major currencies (the dollar, the Euro, the yen), fulfills the functions of a collective colonial monetary authority (for the Triad); the World Bank, which is a sort of Ministry of Propaganda for the G7. Other institutions have charge of the political management of the system; here it is a question in the first place of NATO, which has replaced the UN is speaking on behalf of the world collectivity. The systematic implementation of military control over the planet by the United States expresses quite brutally this imperialist reality. Negri and Hardt's work does not discuss questions relating to the functions of these institutions, no more than it mentions the multiplicity of facts which inconvenience the naive thesis of a "network of power": military bases, powerful interventions, the role of the CIA, etc. The brutality of the U.S. intervention in Iraq makes the whole discourse on "capitalism as a gentle Empire" ridiculous.

In the same manner, the true questions that the technological revolution poses for the system's class structure are evaded in favor of the vague category of the "multitude", the analogue of "the people" of vulgar sociology. The true questions lie elsewhere: how does the technological revolution in progress (whose reality cannot be doubted), like every technological revolution, violently break up the old forms of the organization of work and of the class structure, while the new forms of their recomposition have not yet visibly crystallized?

To crown the whole thing and give a semblance of legitimacy to the imperialist practices of the Triad and the hegemonism of the United States, the system has produced its own ideological discourse, adapted to the new aggressive tasks. The discourse on the "clash of civilizations" is completely intended to cement "Western" racism and cause public opinion to accept the implementation of apartheid on a world scale. This discourse is, in my opinion, far more important than lyrical outbursts about the so-called network society.

The influence which the Empire thesis has gained in the opinion of the Western left, and among youth, derives entirely, in my opinion, from the harsh observations it makes about the state and the nation. The state (bourgeois) and nationalism (chauvinistic) have always been rejected, and rightly so, by the radical left. To assert that, with the new capitalism, there decay is beginning can only be pleasing. But, alas, the proposition is not true. Late capitalism certainly puts on the agenda the objective necessity and possibility of the withering away of the law of value; the technological revolution makes possible, in this context, the development of a network society; the deepening of globalization certainly challenges the existence of nations. But obsolescent capitalism, by means of a violent imperialism, is busily annulling all of the emancipatory possibilities. The idea that capitalism could adapt itself to liberating transformations, that is, could produce them, without wanting to, as well as socialism could, is at the heart of the American liberal ideology. Its function is to deceive us and cause us to forget the extent of the true challenges and of the struggles required to respond to them. The suggested "anti-state" strategy unites perfectly with capital's strategy, which is busy "limiting public interventions" ("deregulating") for its own benefit, reducing the role of the state to its police functions (not at all suppressing the state, but liquidating only political practice, thus allowing it to fulfil other functions). In a similar way, the "anti-nation" discourse encourages the acceptance of the role of the United States as military superpower and world policeman.

Something else is needed: the development of political praxis, granting it its full significance, and the advancement of social and citizen democracy, giving to peoples and to nations greater latitude for action in globalization. Granted, formulas implemented in the past have lost their effectiveness in new conditions. Granted also that certain adversaries of neo-liberal and imperialist reality do not always see that and live on nostalgia for the past. But the whole challenge still remains.

NOTES

1. The author uses two different expressions to represent the concept of alienation in capitalist society: *"l'aliénation marchande"* and *"l'aliénation économiste"*. I have translated both as "economic alienation" for two reasons:
   i. It is a more felicitous expression than the alternatives (e.g., "marketplace alienation" or "commercial alienation" or "economist alienation") and
   ii. It expresses the broadly economic nature of the alienation endemic to capitalist social reality, which owes its specificity to the dominance of the economic and its separation from other aspects of social life.— Trans.

III. The Consequences : Really-Existing Globalized Liberalism

The Para-Theory of Liberalism and its accompanying ideological discourse promise salvation for all of humanity. This promise ignores every lesson of history. Really-existing globalized liberalism can produce nothing other than an intensification of the inequalities between peoples (an intensified global polarization) and within populations (of the global South and North). This pauperization, an integral part of capital accumulation, in turn makes democracy impossible, eliminating its imaginative potential in the developed centers (by substituting a low-intensity democracy for new advances in the social control of transformation) and reducing to farcical status the possible adoption of apparently democratic political forms in the peripheries.

Polarization occupies a central place in the history of the global expansion of really-existing capitalism. I understand by that the continually growing gap between the centers of the global capitalist system and the peripheries. This is a new phenomenon in the history of humanity. The extent of this gap has grown in two centuries to a point where there is nothing in common with what humanity could possibly have experienced in the past. This is a phenomenon that one can only want to do away with by the gradual construction of a postcapitalist society that is really better for all peoples.

Capitalism has developed the productive forces at a pace and to an extent unparalleled in all prior history. But, unlike any prior system, it has simultaneously widened the gap between what this development would potentially allow and the actual use made of that development. Potentially, the level of scientific and technological knowledge attained today makes it possible to resolve all of humanity's material problems. But the logic that transforms the means (the law of profit, accumulation) into an end for itself has, without historical parallel, simultaneously given rise to a gigantic waste of the potential and an inequality of access to the possible benefits. Until the nineteenth century, the gap between the potential development that knowledge made possible and the level of development actually produced was negligible. Not that this reflection should encourage in us any sort of nostalgia for the past: capitalism was a preliminary necessity in order to realize the potential of development attained today. But it has had its day in the sense that continuing to follow its logic would produce no more than waste and inequality. In this context, the "law of immiseration", formulated by Marx, has been verified in a striking manner—on the world scale—every day during the last two centuries. One should not be surprised then that at the very moment when capitalism appears to be completely victorious, the "fight against poverty" has become an unavoidable obligation in the rhetoric of the dominant groups.

This waste and inequality form the dark side of the picture, defining the "black book of capitalism". They remind us that capitalism is only a parenthesis in history and not its end; that if it is not surpassed by the construction of a system that puts an end to global polarization and economic alienation, then it can only lead to the self-destruction of humanity.

The construction of a citizen democracy implies that the advances of socialization be grounded on the implementation of democracy and not exclusively through a market that has never produced the anticipated benefits.

1. FIRST CONSEQUENCE : THE NEGLECTED PAUPERIZATION AND POLARIZATION OF THE WORLD.

Is it poverty or pauperization that is produced by the process of capital accumulation?

It is fashionable today to discourse on poverty and the necessity, if not of eradicating it, at least of reducing its extent. This is a discourse of charity, in the nineteenth century style, which does not devote much time inquiring into the economic and social mechanisms which engender the "poverty" in question, and this in an epoch where the scientific and technological means at the disposal of humanity are sufficient to eradicate it totally.

Capitalism and the New Agrarian Question

All societies prior to capitalism were peasant societies, whose methods of agriculture were certainly diverse. But the logic which defines capitalism (the maximum profitability of capital) was foreign to them all. Capitalist agriculture, represented by a class of newly wealthy peasants, and even owners of modernized latifundia, or by domains exploited by transnational agribusiness corporations, readies the assault on peasant agriculture.

It was given the green flag by the WTO at its meeting in Doha in November 2001. However, at the present time, the agricultural and peasant world still makes up at least one-half of humanity. Its output is divided between two sectors that are economically and socially completely distinct.

Capitalist agriculture, governed by the principle of the profitability of capital, is localized in North America, Europe, the southern cone of Latin America, and Australia, and employs only several dozen million farmers who are not truly "peasants". But their productivity—a function of mechanization (which exists almost exclusively in these regions) and the extent of the land which each possesses—leads to a yield of between 10,000 and 20,000 quintals[1] of grain-equivalents per worker per year.

On the other hand, peasant agricultures support nearly half of humanity—three billion human beings. These agricultures are divided, in turn, between those that have benefited from the green revolution (fertilizer, pesticides, and the best quality seeds), but are still hardly mechanized, whose production yields between 100 and 500 quintals per worker and those that have not benefited from the green revolution, whose production yields only around 10 quintals per worker.

The gap between the productivity of the best equipped agriculture and poor peasant agriculture, which was 10 to 1 before 1940, is today 2000 to 1. In other words, the rate of growth in agricultural productivity has largely surpassed that of other activities, resulting in a real price reduction of 5 to 1.

Capitalism has always combined with its constructive dimension (the accumulation of capital and development of the productive forces) several destructive dimensions, such as the reduction of humanity to being nothing more than the bearer of labour power, itself treated as a commodity; long-term destruction of reliable natural bases for the reproduction of the means of production and of life; and destruction of sections of older societies and sometimes entire peoples, such as the North American Indians. Capitalism has always simultaneously "integrated" (that is, workers subjected to diverse forms of exploitation by expanding capital—by "use" in direct terms) and excluded (that is, those who, having lost the positions that they occupied in older systems, have not been integrated into the new). But in its ascendant, and historically progressive phase, it integrated more than it excluded.

This is no longer the case, as is specifically and dramatically evident in the new agrarian question. If, as dictated by the World Trade Organization since the Doha conference of November 2001, agriculture is integrated into the whole set of general rules of "competition", thereby making agricultural and food products "commodities just like all the others", there will be definite consequences, given the huge conditions of inequality between agribusiness, on the one hand, and peasant production, on the other.

An additional twenty million modern farms, if given the necessary access to important areas of land (taking it away from peasant producers and undoubtedly choosing the best soil) and if given access to the capital markets that would enable them to acquire the proper equipment, could produce enough to replace the peasant production currently purchased by solvent urban consumers. But what would become of the billions of these non-competitive peasant producers? They will be inexorably eliminated over the course of a few dozen years. What is going to become of these billions of human beings, already for the most part the poor among the poor, but who can at least feed themselves, somehow or other, though rather poorly for a third of them (three-quarters of the undernourished in the world live in the rural areas)? Fifty years of any more or less competitive industrial development, even given the fantastic hypothesis of a continual growth of 7 per cent per year for three-fourths of humanity, could not possibly absorb one-third of this reserve. In other words, capitalism is by nature incapable of resolving the peasant question and the only prospect it offers is a planetary shantytown of five billion human beings "too many".

We are thus led to the point where in order to open up a new field for the expansion of capital ("modernization of agricultural production") it would be necessary to destroy—is human terms—entire societies. Twenty million newly efficient producers (fifty million human beings including their families) on one side and five billion excluded on the other. The constructive dimension of this operation represents no more than one drop of water in the ocean of destruction that it requires. I can only conclude that capitalism has entered its declining senile phase; the logic which governs the system is no longer able to assure the simple survival of half of humanity. Capitalism has become barbaric, directly calling for genocide. It is more necessary than ever to substitute for it other logics of development with a superior rationality.

The defenders of capitalism argue that the agrarian question in Europe found its solution through a rural exodus. Why should the countries of the South not reproduce, two centuries later, an analogous model of transformation? It is forgotten here that urban industries and services in nineteenth-century Europe required an abundant labor force and that the excess from this population emigrated en masse to the Americas.

This argument—that the development of capitalism resolved the agrarian question in the centers of the system—has exercised a powerful attraction, even in historical Marxism. Witness Kautsky's celebrated work (*The Agrarian Question*), written prior to the First World War and the bible of social democracy on this question. This point of view was inherited by Leninism and implemented—with dubious results—by means of the politics of "modernization" of collectivized agriculture during the Stalinist period. In fact, if capitalism has truly "resolved" (in its own way) the agrarian question in the centers of the system, in the peripheries, because it is indissociable from imperialism, it has created a new agrarian problem of immense proportions that it is incapable of resolving, except by destroying half of humanity through genocide.

In the Marxist camp, only Maoism grasped the magnitude of the challenge. And that is why those critics of Maoism which see in it a "peasant deviation" prove, by that very assertion, that they do not possess the necessary tools to understand the nature of really-existing (always imperialist) capitalism. They are satisfied with substituting an abstract discourse on the capitalist mode of production in general.

What to do then?

It is necessary to preserve peasant agriculture for the entire visible future of the twenty-first century. This is not for reasons of romantic nostalgia for the past, but quite simply because the solution to the problem is found by going beyond the logic and capitalism and becoming part of the long, secular transition to world socialism. Thus it is necessary to design regulatory policies for the relations between the "market" and peasant agriculture. At the national and regional levels, these regulations, specifically adapted to local conditions, should protect national production, thus assuring the indispensable security of food at the national level and neutralizing the food weapon of imperialism. In other words, delink internal prices from those of the world market—as they should be—by increasing the productivity of peasant agriculture, which is undoubtedly slow, but continual, thereby allowing control over the population transfer from the countryside towards the cities. At the level of what is called the world market, the desirable regulation probably should occur by means of interregional agreements, for example, between Europe, on one side, and Africa, the Arab world, China and India, on the other, thereby responding to the requirements of a development which integrates instead of excluding.

The New Worker Question

The urban population of the planet represents around half of humanity, at least three billion individuals, the other half being peasants. The statistical information concerning this population makes it possible to divide it between what can be called the middle classes and the popular classes.

At the current stage of capitalist evolution, the dominant classes, formal owners of the principal means of production and the senior executive officials who assume managerial responsibility over them, represent only a very small fraction of the global population even if they appropriate a major portion of the revenue available to their societies. This is true even if the middle classes in the older sense of the term—non-wage earners, small business owners, and middle-level managers:

groups that are not necessarily in decline—are added.

But the vast majority of the workers in the modern segments of production are wage earners, making up more than four-fifths of the urban population of the developed centers. This group is divided into at least two categories. The dividing line between them is both visible from the outside for the observer and really lived as such in the consciousness of individuals.

There are those that can be qualified as popular classes in a secure position in the sense that they are secure in their employment, thanks, among other things, to professional qualifications that give them bargaining power with their employers. As a result, these groups are often organized, in certain countries at least, into powerful unions. In every case, these groups carry great political weight which, in turn, strengthens their barganining power.

The others make up popular classes in a precarious position, formed, in part, of wage earners weakened due to their poor bargaining power (resulting from their inadequate qualifications, their status as non-citizens, or their sex, in the case of women) and in part of non-wage earners (officially unemployed, employed in informal sectors). This second category of the popular classes should be qualified as "precarious", rather than as "minimally integrated or nonintegrated" (a fortiori "marginalized"), because these workers are completely integrated into the systemic methods that govern the accumulation of capital.

In tabulating the available information for the developed countries and for certain countries of the South (for which the data are extrapolated), totals are obtained for the proportions that each of the categories defined above represents in the urban population of the planet.

Percentages of the Total Urban Population

	Centers	Peripheries	World
Rich And Middle Classes	11	13	25
Popular Classes	24	54	75
stabilized	(13)	(11)	(25)
precarious	(9)	(43)	(50)
Total	33	67	100
Populations concerned (millions)	(1000)	(2000)	(3000)

Although the centers have only 18 per cent of the planet's population, 90 per cent of that population is urbanized, forming one-third of the world's urban population. If the sum total of the popular classes makes up three-quarters of the world's urban population, the subtotal made by those who are in a precarious position today represents 40 per cent of the center's popular classes and 80 per cent in the peripheries, that is, two-thirds of the popular classes on the world scale. In other words, the popular classes in a precarious position represent at least half of the world's urban population, 80 per cent of them living in the peripheries, in a proportion which amounts to two-thirds of the urban population of the peripheries and one-quarter in the centers.

A look at the composition of the urban popular classes a half century ago, at the end of the Second World War, shows that the proportions which characterized the structure of the popular classes at that time were very different from what they have become. The Third World's portion did not exceed one-half of the global urban population (at that time around one billion individuals) as opposed to two-thirds today. At that time, there were not yet any megalopolises such as are found today in almost any country of the South. There were only a few large cities, notably in China, India, and Latin America.

The popular classes of the centers benefited, after the end of the Second World War, from an exceptional situation based on the historic compromise the working classes forced on capital. This compromise ensured security for the majority of workers in large factories organized on Fordist principles. In the peripheries, the proportion of those in a precarious position was always much larger than in the centers, but did not exceed half of those in the popular classes, as opposed to 70 per cent today. The other half was made up, on the one hand, of those wage-earners securely situated in the new colonial economy and modernized society and, on the other, of those working in older artisanal sectors of the economy.

The major social transformation which characterized the long period of the second half of the twentieth century can be summarized in a single suggestive figure: *the proportion of the popular classes in a precarious position has gone from less than a quarter to more than half of the global urban population and this phenomenon of pauperization has reappeared on a significant scale in the developed centers themselves.* The total number of people in this destabilized urban population has gone in a half century from less than 250 million to more than one and one-half billion individuals, indicating a rate of growth surpassing that of economic or demographic expansion or the movement towards urbanization itself.

There is no better term than "pauperization" to indicate the long-term evolutionary tendency. After all, the fact of poverty itself is recognized and reaffirmed in the new dominant language: reducing poverty has become a leitmotif of the objectives that the ruling powers claim to achieve through the policies that they implement.

But the poverty in question is only presented as a fact which is empirically measured, either very roughly through income distribution (the "poverty threshold") or a little less roughly through composite indices (such as those proposed for "human development" by the UNDP) without posing the question of the methods and mechanisms that generate it.

Our presentation of these same facts goes much further because it enables us to begin explaining the phenomenon and its evolution. Middle classes, secure popular classes and precarious popular classes are all integrated in the same system of social production, but they fulfil distinct functions. Some of them are certainly "excluded" from the benefits of "prosperity", but they are not marginalized in the sense that they are not functionally integrated into the system.

Pauperization is a modern phenomenon (one should speak not of "poverty", but of the "modernization of poverty") that is in no way reducible to having insufficient income to meet the needs of survival. It gives rise to devastating effects in every dimension of social life. Immigrants were completely integrated into the secure popular classes over the course of the "thirty glorious years" (1945–75) as factory workers. However, their children and new arrivals are situated on the margins of the principal productive systems that, in turn, create favorable conditions for replacing class consciousness by "communitarian" solidarities. Women are victims of insecurity more than men, causing their material and social conditions to deteriorate. If feminist movements have undoubtedly realized important advances in the domain of ideas and behaviors, the beneficiaries of these advances are almost exclusively women of the middle classes, certainly not women from the impoverished popular classes. Democracy's credibility, and therefore its legitimacy, is eroded by its incapacity to put a stop to the deteriorating condition of a growing segment of the popular classes.

Pauperization is inseparable from polarization on the world scale, an inherent result of the expansion of really-existing capitalism, which is imperialist by nature. Pauperization of the urban popular classes is closely linked to developments of which the peasant societies of the Third World are victims. The subjection of the latter to the requirements of the expansion of capitalist markets maintains new forms of social polarization which exclude a growing proportion of the peasantry from access to the land. These recently poor or landless peasants fuel the migration toward the shantytowns, more than any demographic growth. All these phenomena are going to worsen as long as liberal dogmas are not called into question and any corrective policy, in this context, would not be able to stop the trend.

Pauperization challenges both economic theory and the strategies for social struggle. Conventional vulgar economic theory evades the real questions posed by the expansion of capitalism. It substitutes the construction of a theory of an imaginary capitalism for the analysis of really-existing capitalism. This imaginary capitalism is conceived as a simple and continual extension of exchange relations ("the market") while the system actually functions and is reproduced on the basis of capitalist relations of production and exchange (not simple commodity relations). This theory then easily makes the assumption that "the market" by itself is self-regulating and produces a social optimum—an assumption that is supported neither by history nor rational argument. "Poverty" can thus be explained only by causes decreed to be external to economic logic, such as demography or policy "errors". Its relationship to the logic of capitalist accumulation is removed from theoretical reflection.

Now this liberal virus, which pollutes contemporary social thought and eliminates the capacity to understand the world, let alone to transform it, has profoundly penetrated the whole of the "historical left" formed in the aftermath of the Second World War. The movements engaged at the present time in social struggles for "another world" (a better one) and an alternative globalization will only be able to produce significant social advances if they get rid of this virus in order to begin an authentic theoretical debate again. As long as they do not rid themselves of this virus, even the best intentioned social movements will remain enclosed in the iron grip of an unchallenged conception and, consequently, prisoners of ineffective propositions about "corrective" measures, such as those that sustain the rhetoric about the "reduction of poverty".

The analysis sketched above should contribute to opening this debate. It reestablishes the relevance of the connection between capital accumulation of the one side and the phenomena of social pauperization, on the other. One hundred and fifty years ago, Marx initiated the analysis of the mechanisms underlying this connection, an analysis which has hardly been pursued since.

2. SECOND CONSEQUENCE: LOW-INTENSITY DEMOCRACY. SOCIALIZATION THROUGH THE MARKET OR THROUGH DEMOCRACY?

Democracy is one of the absolute conditions of social progress, but it should be explained why and under what circumstances. The idea that democracy is such a condition has been generally accepted only for a short period of time. Not so long ago the dominant dogma in the West, as in the East and the South as well, was that democracy was a "luxury" that could thrive only after "development" had resolved the material problems of society. Such was the official doctrine shared by the leadership of the capitalist world (which enabled them to justify their support for military dictators in Latin American and autocratic regimes in Africa), of Third World states (the Latin American theory of underdevelopment or *desarrollismo* clearly expressed this doctrine and single parties were not just the prerogative of socialist states) and of the Soviet system.

Now, overnight, the thesis is turned into its opposite. The concern for democracy has become the object of daily discourse from everyone or almost everyone, the certificate of democratic practice granted in due form as a condition for requesting aid from the rich democracies. This rhetoric is difficult to believe when one knows at what point in practice the "double standards" principle, implemented in perfect cynicism by means of pure and simple manipulation, betrays the actual priority of other unacknowledged objectives.

Democracy is a modern concept in the sense that it defines modernity itself, understood as the adoption of the principle that human beings individually and collectively—that is, socially—are responsible for their history. To be capable of formulating this concept, it is necessary to be liberated from the alienations characteristic of forms of power prior to capitalism, whether they be formulated in religious terms or clothed in other "traditional" forms. In either case, they are conceived as permanent, transhistorical givens. The modernity in question is born with capitalism and the democracy that it produces remains as limited as capitalism is. Its historical bourgeois forms, the only ones known and practiced until today, form only one stage. Neither modernity nor democracy has come to the end of their potential development. Modernity and the democracy that accompanies it do not form a stable state of affairs; they are always essentially incomplete processes. This is the reason why it is preferable to speak of democratization, thereby insisting on the dynamic aspect of an always incomplete process, rather than of democracy, which reinforces the illusion that there can be a definitive formula for it.

Since its origin in the Enlightenment era, bourgeois social thought has been based on a separation among different domains of social life, such as the economic and the political, and the adoption of specific and different principles that express the particular requirements of "Reason" in each of these domains.

In this spirit, democracy would be the reasonable principle of good political management. Since men (it was never a question of women at that time), or more precisely, certain men (sufficiently well-to-do and educated) are reasonable, they should have the responsibility of making the laws under which they want to live and choose (through elections) those who would be responsible for their execution. On the other hand, economic life is managed by other principles equally conceived as the expression of the requirements of "Reason" (seen as synonymous with human nature): private property, the right to make contracts, competition in markets. One can recognize here a group of principles characteristic of capitalism that, by themselves, have nothing to do with principles of democracy. This is even less the case if the latter are conceptualized as implying equality of men, and women as well, of people of all skin colors (remembering that American democracy neglected the slaves until 1865 and the elementary civic rights of their descendants until 1960), of property owners and the propertyless (noting here that private property exists only if it is exclusive, that is, if there are those who do not own property).

From the start, the separation of the economic and political instances poses the question of whether or not the specific logic which governs the economic converges with or diverges from that which governs the political. The self-evident postulate that underlies the currently fashionable discourse asserts that there is a convergence between the two domains. Democracy and the market engender one another, democracy requires the market and vice versa. Nothing is more mistaken than this notion, contradicted by real history.

The Enlightenment thinkers were more demanding than our vulgar contemporaries. They posed the double question: why does this convergence exist and under what conditions? Their response to the first question was prompted by their concept of "reason", the common denominator of modes of governance extolled here and there. If men are reasonable, the results of their political choices can only confirm the results that the market produces on its side. Obviously, this is on condition that the exercise of democratic rights is reserved only to those who are endowed with reason, that is, certain men, not women (who, it is well known, are only emotional and not reasonable), nor slaves, the poor and the deprived (the proletariat), who only obey their instincts. According to this reasoning, democracy must necessarily be restricted, reserved for those who are both citizens and property-owners. Hence it is easily understood how their electoral choices probably always, or almost always, conform to their interests as capitalists. But at the same time, the political loses its autonomy in this convergence with, not to say submission to, the economic. Economic alienation clearly functions here to hide the elimination of the autonomy of the political.

The later extension of democratic rights to others, in addition to citizen-businessmen, was neither the spontaneous product of capitalist development nor a necessity of that development. On the contrary, the extension of these rights was progressively attained by the victims of the system, the working class and later women; it is the result of struggles against the system. By the force of things, this extension of rights could reveal the possible contradiction between the will of the majority—the exploited of the system, expressed through the democratic vote—and the fate reserved for them by the market. The system risks becoming unstable, explosive even. At a minimum, there is a risk, and possibility, that the market will be subject to the expression of social interests that do not correspond with the priority given by the economic to the maximum profitability of capital. In other words, there is a risk for some (capital) and a possibility for others (worker-citizens) of the market being regulated by means that are foreign to the development of its narrow one-sided logic. This is possible, and has happened in certain conditions, such as the postwar welfare state.

But that is not the only possibility of hiding the divergence between democracy and the market. If, in a concrete historical conjuncture, a fragmented movement of social criticism has been weakened because there appears to be no alternative to the dominant ideology, then democracy can be emptied of all content which restricts and is potentially dangerous for the market. It becomes a " low-intensity democracy". You are free to vote as you choose: white, blue, green, pink, or red. In any case, it will have no effect; your fate is decided elsewhere, outside the precincts of Parliament, in the market. The subjection of democracy to the market (and not their convergence) is reflected in political language. The rotation of those in government (but not those in power), always called upon to do the same thing—that is, obey the market—has taken the place of the alternative—that is, a clear choice between socially different options and prespectives. Everything that has been said and written on the double dilution of citizenship and class consciousness into the spectacle of political comedy and the consumption of commodities is contained in this separation between the political and the economic.

This is where we are today. It is a dangerous situation because, with the erosion of the credibility and legitimacy of democratic procedures, it could very well lead to a violent backlash that purely and simply abolishes those procedures altogether in favor of an illusory consensus founded on religion or ethnic chauvinism, for example. In the peripheries of the system, democracy, which is impotent because it is subject to the brutal demands of a savage capitalism, has become a tragic farce, a democracy without value; Mobutu replaced with two hundred Mobutist parties!

The fundamental thesis of bourgeois social thought on the "natural" convergence of democracy and the market carries within it from the very beginning the danger of the trend that confronts us today. It presupposes a society reconciled with itself, without conflict, such as certain so-called postmodernist interpretations propose. Convergence becomes a dogma, a subject about which questions are no longer posed. We are thus no longer in the presence of an attempt to understand, as scientifically as possible, politics in the real world, but a theory of imaginary politics. The latter forms, in its own sphere, the counterpart of "pure economics", which is not the theory of really-existing capitalism, but of an imaginary economy. As soon as the postulate of "reason" as formulated since the Enlightenment era is called into question, as soon as the historical relativity of social rationalities is taken into account, it is no longer possible to accept the commonplaces propagated today about the convergence between democracy and capitalism.

On the contrary, one becomes conscious of the latent authoritarian potential contained in capitalism. The response that capitalism gives to the challenge of the dialectical relationship between the individual and the collective (the social) expresses this dangerous potential, in fact.

The contradiction between the individual and the collective, immanent to every society at all levels of reality, was overcome in all social systems prior to modernity by the negation of the first term, that is, by the domestication of the individual by society. The individual is thus recognizable only by and through his/her status in the family, clan, society. The terms of the negation are inverted in the ideology of the modern (capitalist) world: modernity affirms the rights of the individual over against society. This reversal is only the preliminary condition of a potential liberation, because it simultaneously liberates a potential for permanent aggressiveness in the relations between individuals. Capitalist ideology expresses the reality of this by its ambiguous ethic: long live competition, may the strong win. The devastating effects of this ideology are sometimes limited by the coexistence of other ethical principles, largely of religious origin or inherited from earlier social forms. As these barriers break down, the one-sided ideology of the rights of the individual can only result in horror. There is a striking contrast here between, on the one hand, American ideology which grants to individual liberty an absolute priority over social equality (extreme inequality is, as a result, accepted) and, on the other hand, the European ideology which attempts to link the two themes together without, for all that, being capable, within the context of capitalism, of resolving the contradictions. The attachment of the citizens of the United States to the right to bear arms—with all the well-known disastrous consequences—is the extreme expression of this concept of barbaric liberty.

How will a dialectical synthesis, beyond capitalism, allow the rights of the individual to be reconciled with the rights of the collectivity? How will this possible reconciliation provide more transparency to individual and social life?

Socialization, understood as the reconciliation between the individual and the social, has continually assumed, in history, different forms based on different and unique rationalities. In precapitalist societies it was founded upon the adherence, whether by consent or by force, to common religious beliefs such as personal fidelity to seigniorial and royal dynasties. Socialization in the modern world is founded upon the expansion of capitalist market relations which gradually master all aspects of social life and suppress, or at least largely dominate, all other forms of solidarity (national, familial, communal). This form of socialization "by the market", even if it has enabled a stupendous acceleration in the development of the productive forces, has equally aggravated their destructive characteristics. It tends to reduce human beings to the status of "people" without any identity other than that of being passive "consumers" in economic life and equally passive "spectators" (no longer citizens) in political life. Democracy, which can only be embryonic in these conditions, can and must become the foundation of a completely different socialization, one capable of restoring to the total human being his/her full responsibility in the management of all aspects of social, economic, and political life.

If socialism, the term associated with this perspective, cannot be conceived without democracy, democratization, in a socialist perspective, implies that there is some progress being made in democracy's conflict with capitalist logic. There is no socialism without democracy, no democratic progress without the socialist perspective.

The reader will quickly see the analogy, and not the opposition, between the functioning of the relation between utopian liberalism and pragmatic management in historical capitalism and of the relation between social ideology and actual management in Soviet society. The socialist ideology in question is that of Bolshevism which, on this fundamental point, follows from and does not break with European social democracy prior to 1914. It does not call into question the "natural" convergence between the rationalities of different instances of social life and presents as the "meaning-of history" a facile linear interpretation of its own "necessary" course of action. The convergence is expressed in the same manner: the management of the economy by the plan (substituted for the market) obviously produces, in this dogmatic vision, the adequate response to all needs;

democracy can only support the decisions of the plan and to oppose it is irrational. But here imaginary socialism encounters the demands of the management of really-existing socialism, which is confronted with real and serious problems, such as, among others, developing the forces of production in order "to catch up". Power is attended to by cynical, unavowable, and unavowed practices. Totalitarianism is common to the two systems and is expressed in the same way: by systematic lying. If its manifestations were evidently more violent in the USSR, this is because the developmental delays inherent in the attempt to catch up with the West weighed heavily on the system, while the more advanced state of the West gave its societies a comfortable cushion they could rest on (hence the frequently "soft" totalitarianism, such as in the consumerism of periods of quick and easy growth).

The construction of a society of citizens, of a citizen politics capable of giving a true meaning to democracy, is impossible without breaking from liberal dogma. Getting rid of the liberal virus is an inescapable condition, failing which democracy becomes ridiculous, a means to ensure the one-sided dictatorship of capital.

To abandon the thesis of convergence, of "overdetermination", to accept conflict between the rationalities of different instances, that is, under-determination, is the condition for an interpretation of history that potentially reconciles theory and reality. It is also the condition for the invention of strategies that would grant a real effectiveness to action, that is, enable social progress in every dimension.

NOTES

1. A quintal is equal to 100 kilograms—Trans.

IV. The Origins of Liberalism

1. THE IDEOLOGY OF MODERNITY: THE EUROPEAN VERSION OF THE ORIGIN

Liberal Ideology appears with the rise of modernity and develops simultaneously with the formation of capitalism. All were invented in Europe over the course of three centuries extending from the Renaissance to the French Revolution.

Modernity is the product of a break arising in the history of humanity, a break first beginning in Europe in the course of the sixteenth, seventeenth and eighteenth centuries, but in no way completed, either in its birthplace or elsewhere. The multiple facets of modernity form a whole consonant with the requirements of the reproduction of the capitalist mode of production, but which nevertheless equally allow for the possibility of going beyond the capitalist mode.

Modernity is founded on the demand for emancipation by human beings, beginning with their liberation from the yoke of the social determinations existing in earlier traditional forms of society. This liberation calls for the renunciation of the dominant forms of the legitimization of power—in the family, in communities within which modes of life and production are organized, in the state—based until then on a metaphysics, generally of a religious nature. Modernity implies, then, a break between religion and the state, a radical secularization, which is the condition for the development of modern forms of politics.

The concomitant birth and development of modernity and capitalism are not the products of chance. The social relations characteristic of the new system of capitalist production implied free enterprise, free access to markets, and the proclamation of the untouchable right to private property (which is made "sacred"). Economic life, emancipated from the political power which dominated it in regimes prior to modernity, is made into an autonomous domain of social life, driven by its own laws alone. Capitalism replaces the traditional relation in which power is the source of wealth with the reverse relation which makes wealth the source of power. But so far, really-existing modernity, whose development has remained enclosed within the framework of capitalism, is ambiguous on this question of the relation between power and wealth. In fact, it is based on the separation between two domains of social life, the management of the economy, which is entrusted to the characteristic logics governing the accumulation of capital (private property, free enterprise, competition) and the management of state power by the institutionalized practice of political democracy (rights of the citizen, principles of a multiparty system, etc.). This arbitrary separation vitiates the potential emancipatory power proclaimed by modernity. The modernity that has developed under the limiting constraints of capitalism is, as a result, contradictory, promising much more than it has been able to deliver, thereby creating unsatisfied hopes.

Modernity opens up the possibility for a huge social advance towards the goal of emancipation. The progress of political democracy, as limited as it is, bears witness to this possibility. It has given legitimacy to the action of dominated, exploited, and oppressed classes and enabled them progressively to wrest democratic rights from the power of dominant capital—rights that would never have been spontaneously produced by the logic of capitalist expansion and accumulation. It has released a potential for a political transformation that opens up a wider space for the class struggle, ascribing to the two terms—politics and class struggle—an energizing equivalence in meaning. But, at the same time, it has invented and developed the means that allow it to reduce the potential efficacy of emancipatory democracy.

Simultaneously, capitalism, expanding together with modernity, entails a development of the productive forces to an extent never known before in history. This development allows for the potential resolution of the great material problems of all of humanity. But the logic that governs capitalist accumulation prevents that from happening. On the contrary, it continually deepens a polarization·of wealth to an extent previously unknown in history.

Contemporary people are thus confronted with challenges formed by really-existing capitalism and modernity. The dominant ideology is used simply to avoid awareness of the challenge. Despite the possible sophistication of its language, this ignorance is expressed in a naive manner by the American ideologues of liberalism. This discourse of the self-satisfied acknowledges only a single human value: individual liberty. Such an acknowledgment comes at the price of being unaware that, in the context of capitalism, this liberty allows the strongest to impose their laws on others, that this liberty is completely illusory for the great majority (the liberal hypothesis imagines that each individual can become a Rockefeller just like it was said not long ago that each soldier carried a field marshal's baton in his backpack), that it strikes directly against the aspiration for equality that forms the foundation of democracy.

This same fundamental ideology is shared by all defenders of the system, for whom capitalism is an untranscendable horizon, the "end of history". The more extremist do not hesitate to welcome the concept of society as a jungle of "individuals", to sacrifice the possible pacifying intervention of the state to the principles of an administration which reduces public power to functioning as an instrument at the exclusive service of the "winners". Others wish to give a human face to this dictatorship and attempt to attenuate the extremism of the exclusive principle of individual liberty by diluting it in propositions that associate other pragmatic considerations of social justice with it and by "recognizing differences", such as those among various communities. Postmodernism, by its invitation to "accept" and "adjust to" contemporary reality, to "manage" it by doing only what is immediately possible in the most inspired manner and nothing more, equally evades the challenge.

For the great majority of people, the modernity in question is simple odious, hypocritical, and based on the cynical practice of a double standard. Their rejection is thus violent and this violence is completely legitimate. Really-existing capitalism and the modernity that comes with it have nothing to offer to them.

From the very beginning, capitalism is continually traversed by insurmountable contradictions that call upon us to consider the necessity of surpassing it. This social need is expressed very early and in all the great moments of modern history. It is at work in all three great revolutions of modern times: the French, the Russian, and the Chinese. The French Revolution holds a special place in modern history. The radical Jacobin wing very early recognized the contradictions of bourgeois thought and expressed the essence of those contradictions quite clearly, namely, that economic liberalism is the enemy of democracy. It strove for the triumph of a concept of popular revolution which would go beyond the "objective demands" of the moment—that is, the realization of strictly bourgeois tasks. From this radical current came the first generation of communist critics of nascent capitalism (the Babouvists). In the same way, the Russian and Chinese revolutions went well ahead of the tasks that were immediately imposed on their societies and proposed a communist objective that would largely surpass those immediate tasks. It is not by chance that each of these three great revolutions—contrary to others—was followed by a restoration. The remarkable advances evident in their great moments nevertheless remain living symbols for the future, having put the equality of human beings and their liberation from economic alienation at the heart of their projects. The French Revolution was extraordinarily precocious in this regard.

Generally, the historical conditions that accompanied the development of capitalism in Europe facilitated the ripening of a political class consciousness in the dominated classes. This appeared very early, in the first decades of the nineteenth century, inspired by the most radical advances of the French Revolution. At the end of the century, it inspired the formation of large workers' parties which, over the course of the twentieth century, compelled capital to "adjust" to social claims that did not result from the exclusive logic of capital accumulation. The value "equality" is necessary then as a contradictory complement to the value "liberty".

Economic alienation leads to a privileging of liberty over other human values. Certainly, this is a privileging of individual freedom, but in particular the freedom of the capitalist entrepreneur whose potential is unleashed and whose economic power is increased. By contrast, equality does not arise directly from the requirement of capitalism, except in its most immediate dimension, the (partial) equality of rights that, on the one hand, allows the expansion of free enterprise and, on the other hand, condemns the free worker to submit to wage labor, selling a labor power that is itself a commodity. At a higher level, the value "equality" comes into conflict with "liberty". In the history of part of Europe, if not the whole continent, France in particular, these two values are proclaimed on an equal footing, as in the motto of the Republic. This is not by chance. The origin of this contradictory duality is, in turn, complex. Doubtless one must note the acute struggles of the popular classes as they endeavour to remain autonomous in relation to the ambitions of the bourgeoisie (in the case of the French Revolution this is particularly clear). This contradiction is expressed clearly and openly by the Montagnards who rightly consider that "economic liberalism" (liberty in the American sense of the term) is the enemy of democracy (insofar as the latter is meaningful for the popular classes).

On the basis of this observation, I would venture to explain one of the differences, still visible today, between American society and culture, on the one hand, and European society and culture, on the other. The operation and interests of dominant capital in the United States and in Europe are probably not as different as sometimes suggested (by the well-known opposition between "Anglo-Saxon capitalism" and "Rhenish capitalism"). The conjunction of their interests certainly explains the solidity of the Triad (United States–Europe–Japan) despite the secondary commercial conflicts which can and do oppose one part of the Triad to the others. But the decisions and choices of society, the social projects that inspire the spirit, even implicitly, are fairly different. In the United States, liberty alone occupies the entire field of political values without any problem. In Europe, liberty is always counterbalanced by an attachment to the value of equality with which it must be combined.

American society despises equality. Extreme inequality is not only tolerated, it is taken as a symbol of the "success" that liberty promises. But liberty without equality is equal to barbarism. The many forms of violence that this one-sided ideology produces are not the result of chance and are in no way a ground for radicalization; on the contrary. The dominant culture of European societies has up to the present day combined liberty and equality with less imbalance; this combination, moreover, forms the foundation of the historic compromise of social democracy. Unfortunately, it is true that the evolution of contemporary Europe is tending to bring the society and culture of the continent into harmony with those of the United States, exalting the characteristics of the later into models and objects of an uncritical and overwhelming admiration.

The complex history of Europe finally results in a dual concept articulating the economic, on the one hand, and the political, on the other, into a dialectic that respects the autonomy of each of these two terms. American ideology is unfamiliar with such nuances.

2. AMERICAN IDEOLOGY: UNCOMPROMISING LIBERALISM

This is not the place to examine the complex relations between religions and their interpretations, on the one hand, and the processes of modernization, democracy, and secularization, on the other. I have addressed this subject elsewhere. Thus I will summarize the main conclusions I have reached in the following theses:

Modernization, secularization, and democracy are not the result of an evolution (or revolution) in religious interpretations, but, on the contrary, the latter have accommodated themselves, more or less successfully, to the demands of the former. This accommodation was not the privilege of Protestantism. It worked in the Catholic world in a different way, but it was certainly no less effective. In every case, it created a new religious spirit, freed from dogma.

In this sense, the Reformation was not the condition for the expansion of capitalism, even if Weber's thesis is largely accepted in the societies which it flatters (Protestant Europe). The Reformation was not even the most radical form of the ideological break with the European past and its "feudal" ideologies—among which is the earlier interpretation of Christianity. On the contrary, it was the most confused and primitive form.

There was a "reform by the dominant classes", which resulted in the creation of national churches (Anglican, Lutheran) controlled by these classes. This reform implemented a compromise among the emerging bourgeoisie, the monarchy and large rural property owners, dispelling the threat from the popular classes and from the peasantry, which was regularly subjected to excessive appropriations. This reactionary compromise—which Luther expressed and which Marx and Engels analyzed as such—allowed the bourgeoisies of the countries in question to avoid what happened in France: a radical revolution. Also, the secularization resulting from the implementation of this model has been limited up to the present. The return to the Catholic idea of universality that the national churches represent fulfilled a single function: to seat the monarchy securely, to strengthen the national church's role as the arbitrator between the forces of the ancien regime and the rising bourgeoisie, to reinforce nationalism and to retard the progress of new forms of universalism that socialist internationalism would latter propose.

There were also reformist movements which seized the popular classes, victims of the social transformations caused by the emergence of capitalism. These movements reproduced the older forms of struggle of the millenarian movements of the Middle Ages. They were not ahead of their time, in relation to its demands, but behind it. The dominated classes had to wait for the French Revolution, with its secular popular and radical democratic mobilizations, and then socialism, in order to learn how to express themselves effectively in new conditions. The Protestant sects in question entertained fundamentalist illusions. They created a favorable terrain for the endless reproduction of apocalyptic "sects", as seen in the United States.

The political culture of the United States is not that which took form in France beginning with the Enlightenment and then, above all, during the Revolution and, to various degrees, marked the history of a good part of the European continent. The differences between these two cultures are more than visible. They break out during moments of crisis, resulting in violent oppositions (such as whether or not to respect international legality on the question of the war against Iraq).

Political culture is the product of history viewed over a long period of time which is always, of course, unique to each country. On this level, the history of the United States is marked by specificities which stand out from those that characterize history on the European continent: the founding of New England by extremist Protestant sects, genocide of the Indians, slavery of the Blacks, development of "communitarianism" associated with the successive waves of immigration in the nineteenth century.

The Protestant sects that felt obliged to emigrate from England in the seventeenth century had developed a very particular interpretation of Christianity which they shared neither with Catholics nor the Orthodox nor even—at least to the same extreme degree—with the majority of European Protestants, including, of course, the Anglicans, who were dominant in the ruling class of England. The Reformation as a whole restored the Old Testament, which Catholicism and the Orthodox had marginalized by an interpretation of Christianity that emphasized its break with Judaism rather than its continuity. I return here to what I have written elsewhere on the real or supposed specificities of Christianity, Islam, and Judaism. The current use of the term "Judeo-

Christian", popularized by the expansion of the American Protestant discourse, bears witness to this reversal in the view of the relationship between these two monotheistic religions. The Catholics were won over to this view (but not the Orthodox), not with great conviction, but for reasons of political opportunism.

The Reformation, as we know, was associated with the birth of capitalism in a cause–effect relation that has been interpreted in very different ways in modern social thought. Weber advanced a thesis, which became famous and certainly dominant in the Anglo-Saxon and Protestant world, according to which the Reformation had enabled the growth of capitalism. This thesis was a counterpoint—or wanted to be, I believe—to Marx's thesis that read the Reformation as an effect of transformations caused by the formation of capitalism, from which the various forms of Protestantism grew. Some expressed the protests of the popular classes who were victims of nascent capitalism, while others expressed the strategies of the dominant classes.

In addition, the ideological fragments and value systems that were expressed on this religious terrain retained all the marks of primitive forms of reaction to the challenge of capitalism. The Renaissance went much further in certain respects (Machiavelli is one of the most eloquent witnesses of that). The Renaissance unfolded in Catholic territory (Italy). The management of certain Italian cities as genuine commercial firms directed by a syndicate of the richest shareholders established a purer relation with the first forms of capitalism than was the case between Protestantism and capitalism. (Venice is the prototype of this.) Later, the Enlightenment, which unfolded in Catholic countries (France) as well as in Protestant countries (England, Netherlands, Germany) was situated more in the secular tradition of the Renaissance than in the tradition of religious reform. Finally, the radical character of the French Revolution strengthened the secular, deliberately leaving the terrain of religious reinterpretations behind in favor of grounding itself in modern politics, largely its own creation.

The particular form of Protestantism implanted in New England made a strong impression on American ideology which has continued right up to the present. It was the means through which the new American society began the conquest of the continent, legitimizing it in terms taken from the Bible (the violent conquest by Israel of the Promised Land, an incessantly repeated theme in North American discourse). Thereafter, the United States extended to the whole planet its project of realizing the work that "God" had commanded it to carry out. The people of the United States see themselves as the "chosen people"—a synonym in actual events for *Herrenvolk*, to return to the parallel Nazi terminology. And this is why American imperialism has to be more barbaric than its predecessors, who did not proclaim themselves to have been given a divine mission.

Of course, the American ideology in question is not the cause of the imperialist expansion of the United States. The latter obeys the logic of capital accumulation, whose (completely material) interests it serves. But the ideology is perfectly appropriate. It confuses the issue.

American society is marked right up to the present by the dominance of this sectarian Protestant fundamentalism. This society, as noted by every observer, is preeminently religious, sometimes with a certain naiveté. As a result, it has not been able to establish a strong concept of secularity, which is reduced instead to "tolerance with regard to every religion".

I am not one of those who believe that the past, through force of circumstance, becomes an "atavistic transmission". History transforms people. This is what happened in Europe. Unfortunately, the unfolding of the history of the United States, for from tending to reduce or even obliterate the monstrosity of its origins, has instead favored its expression and perpetuated its effects, whether it be a question of the American Revolution or the populating of the country by successive waves of immigrants.

The American Revolution, much appreciated by many of the revolutionaries of 1789 and today praised more than ever, was only a political revolution with limited social implications. In their revolt against the English monarchy, the American colonists did not want to transform their economic and social relations; they just no longer wanted to share the profits with the ruling class of the mother country. They wanted power for themselves, not in order to create a different society from the colonial regime, but to carry on in the same way, only with more determination and more profit. Above all, their objective was to pursue westward expansion, which implied, among other things, the genocide of the Indians. Maintaining the institution of slavery was not questioned. Almost all of the important leaders of the American Revolution were slave-holding property owners whose prejudices in this regard were resolute.

The genocide of the Indians is naturally a part of the logic of the divine mission of the new chosen people. Do not believe that this belongs entirely to the past. Until the 1960s, responsibility for this genocide was proudly accepted (for example, by means of Hollywood films opposing the cowboy as symbol of Good to the Indian as symbol of Evil) and formed an important element in the education of successive generations.

It is the same with slavery. Almost a century elapsed after independence before slavery was abolished and not for moral reasons, like those invoked during the French Revolution, but only because it was no longer suitable for the pursuit of capitalist expansion. Another century went by before American Blacks attained minimal recognition of some civil rights without disturbing the complete racism of the dominant culture. Until the 1960s, lynchings still occurred. Families went for a "picnic" in order to witness the lynching, sharing in the celebration and exchanging photos of the event. This is perpetuated more discreetly, or more indirectly, by the exercise of "justice" that puts to death thousands of convicts—a disproportionate number of them Blacks. It often comes to light that condemned people are in fact innocent, but this does not necessarily rouse public opinion.

The successive waves of immigration have played a role in reinforcing the American ideology. The immigrants are certainly not responsible for the misery and the oppression that precipitate their departure from their former homes. On the contrary, they are victims. But the circumstances—that is, their emigration—lead them to renounce collective struggles to change the conditions common to their classes or groups in their own countries and result in an adherence to the ideology of individual success in their adopted land. This adherence is encouraged by the American system, to its own advantage. It retards the growth of class consciousness which, having barely begun to mature, must face a new wave of immigrants which, in turn, aborts any political crystallization. But simultaneously this migration encourages the "communitarianization" of American society, because "individual success" does not exclude the inclusion of the immigrant into a community of origin (the Irish, the Italian, etc.), without which the individual's isolation could become unbearable. Here again the reinforcement of this dimension of identity—recuperated and encouraged by the American system—is done to the detriment of class consciousness.

While in Paris the people got ready to begin —"the assault on the heavens" (in the 1871 Commune), in the United States gangs formed by the successive generations of poor immigrants (Irish, Italian, etc.) killed each other, manipulated by the dominant classes with complete cynicism.

The entire difference between the ideology of the United States and that of England or Canada, for example, has its origin here. Protestant Europe—England, Germany, the Netherlands, Scandinavia—shared at the beginning some fragments of an ideology similar to that of the United States, conveyed by the "return to the Bible", though assuredly in attenuated forms rather than the extreme forms found among the sects which emigrated to New England. But in these other countries, the working class succeeded in rising to an assertive class consciousness, while the successive waves of migrants to the United States neutralized that possibility. The emergence of working class political parties made the difference. In Europe, liberal ideology was forcibly combined with other systems of values (including equality, among others) that not only were alien to it, but often in conflict with it. Of course, these combinations have their own history, different from one country and one moment to another. But they did preserve the autonomy of the political moment vis-à-vis the dominant economic one.

Canada, also a young country of immigrants, does not share the American ideology (or not yet?) Because it has not experienced the regular waves of immigrants capable of stifling class consciousness. Maybe it is also because the "loyalists", who did not want to separate from the mother country, did not share the fanaticism of the religious interpretation of the New England sectarians.

In the United States there is no workers' party and there never has been. The trade unions, powerful though they may be, are "apolitical" in all senses of the term. They have no relationship with a political party with which they could form a natural alliance nor are they able to make up for this lack by formulating a socialist ideology themselves. They share the totally dominant liberal ideology with the rest of the society. They continue to struggle on the fixed and limited field of demands that do not challenge liberalism. In a sense, they are "postmodernist" and have always been so.

Communitarian ideologies are not a substitute for a working class socialist ideology, even the most radical among them, such as that elaborated in the Black community. By definition, communitarianism is inscribed within the context of a generalized racism, which it struggles against within the same context, and nothing more.

The combination characteristic of the historical formation of United States society—dominant Biblical religious ideology and absence of a workers' party—has finally produced the unparalleled situation of a de facto single party, the party of capital.

The two segments that form this single party share the same fundamental liberalism. They both appeal only to the minority—40 per cent of the electorate—that participates in the limited and ineffectual democractic life on offer. Each of them has its own clientele—in the middle classes, since the popular classes are much less likely to vote—to which its language is adapted. Each of them crystallizes within itself a conglomerate of segmented capitalist interests (the "lobbies") or "communitarian" supporters.

American democracy constitutes the advanced model of what I call low-intensity democracy. It is based on a total separation between the management of political life, which rests on the practice of multiparty electoral democracy, and the management of economic life, which is governed by the laws of capital accumulation. What is more, this separation is not the object of any radical questioning, but, on the contrary, is part of what is called the general consensus. This separation eliminates all the revolutionary potential of democratic politics. It neutralizes representative institutions (parliament and others), making them impotent in the face of the dictates of the market. Vote Republican, vote Democrat, it makes no real difference when your future does not depend on your electoral choice but on the uncertainties of the market.

Clearly, Europe is not protected from an impoverishing trend of this nature. With the winning over of socialist parties to liberalism and the crisis in the world of labor, Europe is already well involved in such a trend. But it should be able to extricate itself.

The American state is at the exclusive service of the economy—that is to say, it is a faithful servant of capital, without having any concern for other social interests. This is because the historical formation of American society has blocked the maturation of a political class consciousness among the popular classes.

As a counterpoint, the state in Europe has provided (and could provide again) the necessary mediating structure for the confrontation among social interests and, on that basis, has promoted historical compromises that give meaning and real scope to democratic practice. If the State is not compelled to fulfil this function by class and political struggles that maintain their autonomy in relation to the exclusive logic of capital accumulation, then democracy becomes a derisory practice, as it is in the United States.

It is within this context that it is necessary to examine in action this curious democracy, supposedly the oldest and most advanced.

The United States invented the presidential system. It is possible that at the time the self-evident idea of a monarch, even if elected, seemed to be indispensable. Yet the French Revolution had no problem doing without it between 1793 and 1798. The presidential system has always been a catastrophe for the radicalization of democracy and that is truer today than ever before.

The presidential system tends to displace political debate, to weaken it by substituting for a choice of ideas or programs a choice between individuals, even if they supposedly incarnate these ideas or programs. What is more, the always fatal reduction of the choice to two individuals accentuates the search by each of them for the largest consensus (the battle to gain the undecided center, the least politicized) to the detriment of radicalization. This gives a premium to conservatism.

This presidential system, conservative by nature, was exported by the United States to all of Latin America without difficulty, mainly because the political revolutions in the latter, at the beginning of the nineteenth century, were limited and of the same nature as in the United States. The presidential system was a perfect fit. It has subsequently conquered Africa and a good part of Asia for analogous reasons, stemming from the limited character of the national liberation movements of the recent past.

It is also in the process of conquering Europe, where, however, it has left only a detestable memory among democrats, having been associated with the demagogic populism of bonapartism. France, alas, initiated the movement with the creation of the Gaullist republic which does not represent a step forward in the progress of democracy but a retreat into which French society seems to have settled. The arguments invoked to justify this move concern the instability of governments in parliamentary regimes and are purely opportunist.

The presidential system equally favors the crystallization of diverse interest groups—ideally into two groups aligned behind the leading presidential contenders—to the detriment of the formation of authentic political parties (including socialist parties), potential carriers of truly alternative social projects. Here again the case of the United States is exemplary. There are not really separate Democrat and Republican parties. Julius Nyerere said, not without humor, that it is a question of "two single parties". That is a good definition of low-intensity democracy. After all, this situation is understood as such by the popular classes in the United States who often do not vote because they sense—rightly—that the process is meaningless.

Far from being an instrument of eventual social radicalization, the forms of American democracy were and are perfectly convenient forms for conservatism. In these conditions, the other dimensions of American democracy, also often judged positively, are transformed into their opposites. The "decentralization", for example, associated with the increase in authority entrusted to locally-elected powers grants a premium to local notables and to the "communitarianist" spirit. In France as well, the regional powers always or almost always prove to be to the right of the national power—and not by chance.

The absence of permanent bureaucracies in the United States, what liberals believe to be an advantage over the solid implantation of the bureaucratic heritages of Europe, becomes the means by which conservative political power entrusts the implementation of its programs to irresponsible transitory officials who are recruited largely from among the business community (and thus are both regulators and those who are to be regulated). Is this truly an advantage? And whatever one says about *l'Énarchie* in France[1]—about which many of the critiques are justified—is not the idea of a bureaucracy recruited in an authentically democratic manner better (or less bad) until such time as we attain the distant ideal of a society without a bureaucracy?

The unreflective critique of "bureaucracy", which is part of the current received wisdom, directly inspires the systematic campaigns against even the idea of public services, which according to this critique, should be replaced by private services provided by the market. An objective look at the real world demonstrates the public service (supposedly "bureaucratized") is not as inefficient as often supposed, as perfectly illustrated by comparing the United States with Europe in the area of health care. In the United States, health care (largely privatized) costs the nation 14 per cent of its GDP, as opposed to 7 per cent in Europe (where health care is largely provided by public services). In terms of results (quality of health), the comparison favors Europe. But obviously the profits of the pharmaceutical and insurance oligopolies are mainly much higher in the United States than in Europe. Moreover, in a democracy, public service is at least potentially susceptible to transparency. A privatized service, protected by the "secrecy of business matters", is by definition opaque. The substitution of privatized services (socialization by the market) for public services (socialization by democracy) is used as a means to consolidate the consensus that the economic and the political are two rigidly separate spheres. This consensus is destructive of all potential radicalization of democracy.

The "independent" judiciary and the principle of elected judges have demonstrated how they could, in their way, encourage the entrenchment of always conservative, even reactionary, prejudices, and not favor radicalization, in fact form an obstacle to it. The model is nevertheless in the process of being imitated elsewhere (in France, for example; with immediate results that I will refrain from commenting upon).

Besides, the dossier of American justice is there to demonstrate the derisory character of the democracy that it is supposed to serve. This is a justice that is onerous in the extreme, an *a la carte* justice, interpreting in its own way the English *Common Law* from which it is descended, always at the service of the exclusive principles of liberalism (hence of the rich). It is an extremely brutal and systematically racist justice (a large proportion of condemned Blacks are subsequently found to be innocent). The United States has the highest proportion of incarcerations in the world.

The Dreyfus affair mobilized—and divided—all of French society and the French political world. In the

United States, the murders of Sacco and Vanzetti, the Rosenbergs, and many others less well known never roused public opinion to the same degree. There will never be a rehearing. There is neither the right—nor even the idea—of calling into question the injustice of the judges. In addition, the judges, "independent of the State" but subject to a manipulable electorate, are not even obligated by formal written legislation, which they then would only apply, as is the case on the European continent and, in principle at least, in the majority of countries in the world. The judge "creates the law"—a principle found in forms of law in primitive societies, surpassed elsewhere. In these conditions, the decisions of the Court are almost always known in advance. It is well known that the Supreme Court ratified the electoral fraud which allowed Bush Jr. to gain the Presidency, because there was a Republican majority on the Court, which "judged in good conscience" (!) without being accountable to a text which would obligate them to annual votes when the ballot boxes had been recovered—in broad daylight! The same practices of "justice" are quite simply qualified as nepotism when they are done by regimes which make no claim to be democratic.

WHAT IS THERE TO BE ENVIOUS OF IN THIS MODEL?

The combination of a dominant religiousness exploited by a fundamentalist discourse and the absence of political consciousness among the dominated classes gives to the system of power in the United States an unparalleled margin of maneuver. Hence the potential significance of democratic practices is eliminated and they are reduced to the status of harmless rituals (political spectacle, the inauguration of electoral campaigns by marching majorettes, etc.).

But let there be no mistake here. It is not the supposedly religious fundamentalist ideology that is in command and imposes its logic on the true holders of power—capital and its servants in the State. It is capital alone that makes all the appropriate decisions and then afterwards mobilizes the American ideology in question to serve it. The means utilized—unparalleled systematic disinformation—are thus effective, isolating critical thinkers, subjecting them to constant, hateful blackmail. Power then succeeds, with no difficulty, in manipulating an "opinion" held together by its foolishness.

The ruling class of the United States has developed, in these circumstances, a complete cynicism, disguised by a degree of hypocrisy that every foreign observer notes, but that the American people never see! The use of violence, in extreme forms, is implemented every time it is necessary. All the radical American militants know it: to sell out or be murdered is the only choice left to them.

The American ideology, like all ideologies, is "worn away by time". In "calm" periods of history—marked by strong economic growth accompanied by satisfactory social effects—the pressure that the ruling class must exert on its people is weakened. From time to time, then, according to the needs of the moment, this ruling class "reinvigorates" American ideology by means which are always the same: an enemy (always external, American society being declared good by definition) is designated (the Empire of Evil, the Axis of Evil) enabling the "mobilization" of every means destined to eliminate it. Yesterday it was communism, which, through

McCarthyism (forgotten by the "pro-Americans"), made the Cold War possible as well as the subordination of Europe. Today it is "terrorism", an obvious pretext (September 11 strongly resembles the Reichstag fire in this respect), which causes the real project of the ruling class to be overlooked: securing military control of the planet.

The avowed objective of the new hegemonist strategy of the United States is not to tolerate the existence of any power capable of resisting the injunctions of Washington. To carry out that objective, it seeks to dismantle every country that is deemed to be "too large", so as to create the maximum number of failed States, easy prey for the establishment of American bases ensuring their "protection". Only one state has the right to be "great", the United States, according to the last three presidents (Bush Senior, Clinton, Bush Junior).

It is not difficult to be aware of the objectives and means of Washington's project. They are the object of an ostentatious display whose principal virtue is its frankness, even though the legitimization of the objectives is always embedded in a moralizing discourse characteristic of the American tradition. The American global strategy pursues five objectives:

1. To neutralize and subdue the other partners in the Triad (Europe, U.S.A., Japan) and minimize their capacity to act outside of American control.
2. To establish military control through NATO and "Latin Americanize" the former parts of the Soviet world.
3. To establish undivided control of the Middle East and Central Asia and their petroleum resources.
4. To dismantle China, ensure the subordination of other large states (India, Brazil) and prevent the formation of regional blocs which would be able to negotiate the terms of globalization.

5. To marginalize regions of the South that have no strategic interest for the United States.

Thus, the hegemonism of the United States rests far more on its excessive military power than on the "advantages" of its economic system. I will be satisfied with summarizing the import of the arguments I have dedicated to this question elsewhere by accentuating the real political advantage possessed by the United States: it is one state, Europe is not. It can thus play the part of the uncontested leader of the triad by making its military power and NATO, which it dominates, the "visible fist" charged with imposing the new imperialist order on possible recalcitrants.

The military power of the United States has been systematically constructed since 1945, covering the entire planet which is divided into regions based on the integrated system of U.S. military commands. Until 1990, this hegemonism was forced to accept the peaceful coexistence imposed on it by Soviet military power. This is no longer the case. One can only note here the contrast between the planetary vocation of the military strategy of the United States since 1945 and the defensive strategy of the Soviet Union, which never had an offensive strategy aimed at "conquering the world in the name of communism", as Western propaganda—alas, all too successfully—pretended.

The period is therefore characterized by a retreat from democracy, not by an advance towards it. On the global level since the 1980s, with the collapse of the Soviet system, a hegemonist option has been designed which has won over the whole of the ruling class of the United States. Carried away by intoxication with their military power, henceforth without any competition, the United States has chosen to assert its domination straight away by the deployment of a strictly military strategy for control of the planet. The accompanying political strategy prepares the pretexts for it, whether that be terrorism, the fight against the drug trade, or the accusation of producing weapons of mass destruction.

"Preventive war", which Washington reserves to itself as a "right" to invoke, directly eliminates international law. The Charter of the United Nations prohibits recourse to war except in cases of legitimate self defense and subjects possible military intervention by the U.N. to strict conditions, the response having to be cautious and provisional. Every jurist knows that the wars undertaken since 1990 are completely illegitimate and thus in principle those who are responsible are war criminals. The United Nations is already treated by the United States, with the complicity of others, like the League of Nations was treated by the fascist states not long ago.

The abolition of peoples' rights is already underway. The principle of equality among people has been replaced by the distinction between a "master race" or *Herrenvolk*— the people of the United States and, behind them, the people of Israel—and other peoples. This "Master Race" has the right to conquer "the living space" deemed necessary, while the very existence of other peoples is tolerated only if it does not constitute a threat to the ambitions of those called upon to be the "masters of the world". Hence, in the eyes of the Washington establishment, we have all become "redskins", that is, peoples that have a right to exist only in so far as we do not obstruct the expansion of the transnational capital of the United States.

What are the "national" interests that the ruling class of the United States reserves to itself the right to invoke as it sees fit? To tell the truth, this class recognizes only one objective: "to make money". The U.S. state openly gives top priority to satisfying the demands of the transnationals, the dominant segment of capital.

This project is certainly imperialist in the most brutal sense, but it is not "imperial" in the sense that Negri gives to the term, because it is not a question of governing all of the world's societies in order to integrate them into a coherent capitalist system, but only of pillaging their resources. The reduction of social thought to the basic axioms of vulgar economics, the one-sided attention given by dominant capital to the maximization of financial profitability in the short term, reinforced by the well-known inclination to use military means to that end, are responsible for this barbaric turn of events, an inherent tendency of capitalism. It has gotten rid of all systems of human values and replaced them with the exclusive requirements associated with submitting to the so-called laws of the market.

The project has nothing to do with the extension of democracy (even under its American form) to the whole world, as the dominant media pretend. It is not a question of democratizing Iraq or any other country in the region (after all, Israel does not want that), but simply of pillaging their wealth (under the circumstances, Iraqi petroleum). The United States has occupied Kuwait for a dozen years: has it promoted any democracy whatsoever? The only legislative initiative of American Kuwait was to curtail freedom of expression even more by simply prohibiting any criticism of the United States!

For the Arab World, Washington's project does not promote any democratic advances. On the contrary, it aims to replace the current regimes with "Islamic" dictatorships no less violent, but friendly and submissive.

In some way, this would allow for reconciliation between the Saudi project and Washington. In turn, these Islamic regimes will one day undoubtedly be encouraged to make themselves popular by supporting acts of terrorism, but this time against different states (against France, Germany, Russia, and China, for example).

Everyone knows that this strategy suits Israel's purpose, which does not hide its rejection of genuine Arab democracies, supported by their peoples, because democratic Arab countries would modify the balance of forces in favor of the Palestinian cause. As for the promises made by Bush Jr. to "settle—after the victory in Iraq—the Palestinian problem" they resemble very much the lies of Bush Sr., who made the same promise in 1991, in order to be taken seriously.

In the domestic sphere, the retreat of democracy is no less visible. The FBI–CIA–Gestapo is henceforth authorized not to respect any of the most elementary human rights in its prisons and torture centers at Guantanamo, Barmak, and elsewhere tomorrow.

In moments like this, the society of the United States buries itself in its tradition of apocalyptic vision. There is a flourishing of sects whose discourses and practices are well known, a fascist-type popular mobilization. Fools of God and simultaneously fools of the market, these two fundamentalisms unproblematically complement each other here.

Neither this project of the ruling class of the United States nor the American ideology that supports it is "invincible". If it should happen that this project were to be deployed for a certain period of time, it would only lead to a growing chaos that, bit by bit, would require more and more brutal methods of control, without any long term strategic vision. If need be, Washington will no longer seek to strengthen its real allies, which always implies knowing how to make concessions. Puppet governments, like that of Karzai in Afghanistan, are better for business, while the delirium of military power makes it possible to believe in the "invincibility" of the United States. Hitler did not think otherwise.

More precisely, one of the major weaknesses of American thought, resulting from its history and its ideology, is that it has no long-term vision. This thought is embedded in the immediate about which it collects an alarmingly large quantity of data. It believes that it can clarify its immediate choices exclusively through the analysis of the "present", always judging the "past" as irrelevant (the expression "it is history" is an American synonym for "without importance"). The future, in these conditions, is always conceived as the simple projection of the immediate. This is what explains the popularity of idiotic texts like Huntington's work *The Clash of Civilizations*. Using the same method, a writer who would have been alive during the religious wars of the sixteenth century would have concluded that Europe was condemned to self-destruction or at least that one of the two camps (Protestant or Catholic) would succeed in dominating the whole continent.

The idea that history is punctuated by ruptures, produced by the exacerbation of the contradictions that drive it, is foreign to American thought. Foreign also is the idea that historical evolution sets out again from these periods in a direction that is not inherent in any projection of the past into the present.

This is why American imperialism will be infinitely more barbaric than were the earlier forms of European imperialism. Beyond the interests of capital for which their states took responsibility while involved in imperial adventures, the British and French possessed intellectual means enabling them to "think about Empire in the long term". The comparison between what they built on the African continent—as unacceptable as it was—and the total failure of Washington in administering its mini-colony (Liberia) is testimony to the poverty of American political thought. The sole principle and objective guiding Washington in its new imperial policy is immediate pillage. Fifteen million dollars of immediate extra profits (by pillaging the petroleum resources of some countries, for example) against three hundred million victims, with all that holds for the future: the choice will be for the immediate advantage.

American ideology and thought are not exportable. Despite the successes of "Americanization", a salutary reaction to it has begun to appear in European thought, motivated by the absurd and directionless violence produced by the American project ("permanent war").

The militarist option of the United States threatens everyone. It arises from the same logic as Hitler's: to change economic and social relations in favor of the current chosen people *(Herrenvolk)* through military violence. This option, by forcibly occupying center stage, overdetermines every political conjuncture because its pursuit renders every advance that people could obtain from their social and democratic struggles extremely precarious. To bring the militarist project of the United States to defeat has become the primary task, the major responsibility, for everyone.

The United States is the preeminent rogue state, as William Blum has written. It has openly repudiated all respect for legality and for the rights of others, proclaiming their adherence to the single principle that "might makes right". That a regime governed by the political mechanisms of democracy again takes up, to its advantage, the principle proudly held by the Nazis is not an attenuating circumstance, but, on the contrary, makes it even more heinous.

Certainly, the fight to defeat the project of the United States will take many forms. It requires diplomatic aspects (the defense of international law), military aspects (the rearmament of every country in the world in order to meet any aggression contemplated by Washington is imperative; never forget that the United States utilized nuclear weapons when it had a monopoly of them and renounced their use when it no longer had such a monopoly), and political aspects (notably in reference to building a European presence and reconstructing a nonaligned front).

The success of this struggle will depend on the ability of people to liberate themselves from liberal illusions. There will never be an "authentically liberal" globalized economy. Nevertheless, one is tempted and will continue to be tempted, by every means, to believe it. The World Bank has no other function than to operate as a sort of ministry of propaganda for Washington with its treatises on "democracy", "good governance", and "reduction of poverty". For example, there was the media noise organized around Joseph Stiglitz, who discovered some elementary truths, which he asserted with arrogant authority, without, however, calling into question the tenacious prejudices of vulgar economics. The reconstruction of a front from the South capable of giving to the solidarity of Asian and African people, to the three southern continents as a whole, an ability to act on the global level will only happen through liberation from the illusions of a "non-asymmetric" globalized liberal system which ostensibly enables Third World nations to overcome their developmental "delays". Is it not ridiculous to see the countries of the South clamoring for the "implementation of the principles of liberalism but without any discrimination", thereby gaining the full praise of the World Bank? Since when has the World Bank defended the Third World against the United States?

Undoubtedly, a certain number of Third World governments are odious. But the path towards necessary democratization surely does not lie in replacing them with puppet governments that arrive in the wake of the invader, delivering the resources of their countries to pillaging by American transnationals.

The fight against the imperialism of the United States and its militarist option is everyone's—its major victims in Asia, Africa and Latin America, the Japanese and European peoples condemned to subordination, even the North American people. We salute here the courage of all those in "the belly of the beast" who refuse to submit just like their predecessors who refused to surrender to McCarthyism in the 1950s. It is only when the project of its ruling class is defeated that the way will be open to the people of the United States to escape from its ideology.

Will the dominant class in the United States be capable of renouncing the criminal project to which it has rallied? This question is not easy to answer. Possibly political, diplomatic, and even military defeat could encourage the minority at the heart of the U.S. establishment who would agree to renounce the military adventures in which their country is engaged.

The deviation of the United States has been amply encouraged by the choices of European governments all through the 1990s. The Soviet collapse, far from being the occasion for the majority of the European left (socialists had assumed governmental responsibilities in almost all of the countries in the European Union) to reformulate an appropriate European social model, instead saw them carried away with the liberal delirium and aligning themselves with Washington's hegemonist project. These governments bear a heavy responsibility towards history for this behaviour. They ratified Washington's proposals, which made NATO the instrument of its aggressive designs. By associating themselves with the violation of international law, they offered Bosnia, Kosovo, Macedonia, and beyond that every country of Eastern Europe to Washington on a silver platter. Thus during the entire decade they favored the implementation of the American plan for military control of the planet, beginning with the Balkans–Middle East–Central Asian region.

Encouraged by these successes, the American extreme right has succeeded in taking the reins of power in Washington. From now on the choice is clear: accept the hegemonism of the United States and a strengthened liberal virus, reduced to the exclusive principle of "making money", or reject both. The first alternative confers on Washington the major responsibility of remaking the world in the image of Texas. The second is the only one that can contribute to the rebuilding of a plural, democratic, and peaceful world.

Today the United States is governed by a junta of war criminals who came to power through a quasi-coup d'etat, following questionable elections (at least Hitler was truly elected!). After its Reichstag fire (September 11), this junta gave powers to its police similar to those given to the Gestapo. The junta has its *Mein Kampf*, its mass organizations and its preachers. It is necessary to have the courage to speak all of these truths and hereafter stop hiding them behind the insipid and derisory phrase, "our American friends . . ."

If Europeans had reacted in 1935 or 1937, they would have succeeded in stopping the Hitlerian madness. By reacting only in September 1939, they allowed dozens of millions of victims to have that madness inflicted on them. We must act sooner rather than later to face the challenge of Washington's neo-nazis.

NOTES

1. *L'Énarchie* is a term used to refer collectively to students and graduates of the prestigious *École nationale d'administration* (ENA), which educates most of the government officials in France. It is associated with a particular political and cultural style, in the eyes of its critics.—Trans.

V. The Challenge
of Liberalism Today

Today, Liberalism is a Grave Challenge to all of humanity, threatening it with self-destruction. At the same time, globalized liberalism can only reinforce the hold of American imperialism on the whole of the planet. It subordinates Europe and, using historically unprecedented and savage methods, subjects the rest of the world to pillage, including genocide if necessary.

This challenge will be presented here in three sections.

1. FIRST CHALLENGE: REDEFINE THE EUROPEAN PROJECT (AT LEAST FOR SOME EUROPEANS)

Every European government has, up to now, rallied around the theses of liberalism. This winning over of the European states means nothing less than the disappearance of the European project, through a double dilution: economic (the advantages of the European economic union are diluted in economic globalization) and political (European political and military autonomy disappears). There is no longer, at present, a European project. A North Atlantic project (or possibly a project of the Triad) under American command has replaced it. This latter project, which had been suggested earlier by a European commissioner, Léon Brittain, and created a general outcry at the time (at least in France) is, in fact, the only one implemented at the present time.

The hegemonism of the United States is clearly visible behind the disappearance of the European project in favor of a return to Atlanticism. All the same, the decline of this project should be problematic for at least some sectors of public opinion and some segments of the political classes in certain European countries, France in particular. The themes surrounding the formation of a European project had been associated with wealth, power, and independence, to such an extent that it is bound to be difficult to swallow the pill—that is, to accept that United States military "protection" is even more necessary today than yesterday!

The "made in USA" wars have certainly awakened public opinion—everywhere in Europe against the latest of these in Iraq—and even certain governments, first of all France, but also Germany, Russia, and, beyond that, China. It remains true that these governments have not called into question their faithful adherence to the demands of liberalism. This major contradiction will have to be overcome one way or another, whether by submitting to Washington's demands (which a different set of leaders than the ones surrounding Bush Jr. could "facilitate" by the adoption of less arrogant attitudes) or by a true rupture which would put an end to Atlanticism. Will this be possible on the European scale as a whole? Or will it lead to rethinking the project in terms that would allow the nation states that make up the continent to conserve their political autonomy ("the Europe of Nations," return to General de Gaulle's terms)? A diplomacy of varying configurations, associating Paris,

Berlin, Moscow (and later Peking), would complement the latter possibility by widening the margins for the economic autonomy of Europe as a whole. If these choices are not laid out more clearly, European people will remain prisoners of the shifting sands of the European project.

The major political conclusion that I draw from the analysis outlined here is that Europe cannot make different choices as long as the political alliances that define the power blocs remain centered on dominant transnational capital. If social and political struggles can modify the alliances that define these blocs and impose a new historic compromise between capital and labor, then Europe would be able to distance itself more from Washington. That, in turn, would allow the renewal of a possible European project. In these conditions, Europe could—should even—disassociate itself on the international plane from the exclusive demands of a collective imperialism in its relations with the East and the South. Such a move would begin Europe's participation in the long march "beyond capitalism". In other words, Europe will be left (the term left being taken seriously here) or it will not be.

To reconcile loyalty to liberalism with the assertion of political autonomy for Europe or for the States that make up Europe remains the objective of certain fractions of the European political classes who are anxious to preserve the exclusive position of large capital. Will they succeed? I very much doubt it.

At the same time, will the popular classes in Europe, here and there at least, be able to overcome the crisis that seriously affects them, whose features we have attempted to outline above? I believe this is possible, precisely for reasons that I likewise alluded to and which would make it possible for the political culture of certain European countries at least, which is different from that of the United States, to bring about this renaissance of the left. Obviously, the necessary condition is to be liberated from the virus of liberalism.

I use the terms "Europe" and "European project" here because they are the ones which are actually employed on the political scene. But they are subject to entirely unavoidable questions. What does the "European project" consists of and whose interests does it serve? Is this project possible? If not, what alternative can one conceive and propose?

Conceived at the end of the Second World War, the "European project" was born as the European part of the Atlanticist project of the United States, in the spirit of the Cold War initiated by Washington. This is a project which the European bourgeoisies—at the time weak and afraid of their own working classes—adhered to practically without condition. This is still largely true, as seen in the choices put into effect by the ruling classes and the political forces of the right and the majority left, at least in certain European countries, above all in Great Britain, where it is done clearly and ostentatiously. In other countries there is perhaps a bit more hesitation, while in Eastern Europe the process in managed by political classes formed in the culture of servility.

However, the actual implementation of this project—even if the project itself has questionable origins—has progressively modified the important particulars of the problem and the challenges. Western Europe has succeeded in overcoming its economic and technological backwardness in relation to the United States, or at least has the means to do so. In addition, the "Soviet enemy" (and its possible communist allies inside certain European societies) no longer exists. Besides that, the unfolding of this project has eclipsed the most important violent conflicts which had marked a century and a half of European history: the three major countries of the continent—France, Germany, and Russia—have reconciled. All of these changes are, in my opinion, positive and potentially even more positive. Certainly, the implementation of this project has been grounded on economic bases inspired by the principles of liberalism, but a liberalism that was tempered up until the 1980s by the social dimension. The latter was taken into account by and through the "social democratic historical compromise" that forced capital to accommodate the demand for social justice expressed by the working classes. Since then, this project has been pursued in a new social context inspired by American-style liberalism, which is antisocial.

This latest turn has plunged European societies into a multidimensional crisis. First of all, there is the economic crisis as such, inherent in the liberal option. This crisis is aggravated by the willingness of the European countries to align themselves with the economic demands of the North American leader by consenting, up until now, to finance the latter's deficit to the detriment of its own interests. Then there is a social crisis that is accentuated by the growing resistance and struggles of the popular classes against the fatal consequences of the liberal option. Finally, there is the beginning of a political crisis centered on the refusal to be aligned, at least unconditionally, with the current choice of the United States: unending war against the South.

How do the European people and states meet this triple challenge? And will they do so?

The "pro-Europeans" (or, as we might call them, Europeanists of principle) are divided into four fairly different groups:

1. Those who defend the liberal option and accept the leadership of the United States, almost without condition.
2. Those who defend the liberal option but desire a politically independent Europe, freed from alignment with the Americans.
3. Those who desire (and fight for) a "social Europe", that is, a capitalism tempered by a new social compromise between capital and labor operating on a European scale, without being too concerned about Europe's foreign policy in relation to the rest of the world.
4. Finally, those who articulate their demand for a social Europe by constructing a political Europe which practices a "different relationship" (by implication, friendly, democratic, and peaceful) with the South, Russia, and China.

Further, there are indeed "non-Europeans" in the sense that they do not think that any of the four pro-European options are desirable or even possible. They are still, for the moment, strongly in the minority, but certainly gathering strength. Moreover, they are getting stronger in one of two fundamentally different forms: a right-wing "populist" form that rejects the gradual development of supranational political—and maybe economic—power, except obviously for the power of transnational capital; and a left-wing popular form that is national, citizenly, democratic, and social.

Which forces do each of these tendencies rely upon and what are their respective chances of success?

Dominant capital is liberal by nature. As a result, it is inclined, logical enough, to support the first of the four options. Tony Blair represents the most coherent expression of what I have called "the collective imperialism of the Triad". Just as yesterday entire sections of large capital were arrayed behind Hitler out of fear of communism, today the unconditional defenders of the collective imperialism of the Triad believe it necessary to support Bush. In this sense, Tony Blair is not Churchill, who chose to reject Hitler. He resembles rather Chamberlain who considered himself obliged, because of faint-heartedness, to make necessary concessions to Hitler or Mussolini, who intended to make the best of his joining the most powerful. Today, to compare Saddam Hussein to Hitler is to dignify a joke. One could quibble for a long time to decide whether Saddam or Bush is the most odious person. But if there is a power that threatens all of humanity, it is certainly the United States, not Iraq. The political class that has rallied behind the star-spangled banner is disposed, if necessary, to "sacrifice the European project"—or at least to dissipate all illusions on the subject—by keeping it within the constraints of its origins: to be the European wing of the Atlanticist project. But Bush, like Hitler, does not conceive of allies as other than subordinates who are unconditionally aligned with him. That is the reason why important segments of the political class, including the right—even though they are in principle defenders of the interests of dominant capital—refuse to be aligned with the United States, just like earlier with Hitler. If a Churchill is possible in Europe, it would have to be Chirac. Will he be one?

This strategy could successfully be accommodated by an "anti-Europeanism of the right", which would then be satisfied with demagogic nationalist rhetoric (for example, mobilizing the issue of immigration—from the South, of course) whereas in fact it would be subject to the demands of a liberalism that is not specifically "European", but globalized. Aznar and Berlusconi are prototypes of this type of Washington ally, as are the servile political classes of Eastern Europe.

Therefore, I believe that the second option is difficult to maintain. It is, however, that of major European countries—France and Germany. Does this option express the ambitions of a capital that is powerful enough to be above to emancipate itself from the supervision of the United States? This is a question to which I have no answer. It is possible, but intuitively I would say that it is not very probable.

Nevertheless, this is the choice of allies facing a North American adversary which is the principal enemy of all of humanity. I speak indeed of allies because I am convinced that, if they persist in their choice, they will be led to end their subjection to the unilateral project of capital (liberalism) and to look for alliances on the left (the only ones which can lend strength to their project of independence vis-à-vis Washington). An alliance among groups two, three, and four is not impossible, just like it was with the great anti-Nazi alliance.

If this alliance takes form, then should it and will it be able to operate exclusively within the European framework, all the Europeanists being incapable of renouncing the priority given to this framework? I do not believe it, because this framework, such as it is and will remain, systematically favors only the option of the first group, the pro-American group. Would it be necessary then to break up Europe and definitively renounce its project?

I do not believe that would be either necessary or even desirable. Another strategy is possible: leave the "sclerotic" European project, for a time, at its present stage of development and, parallel to that, develop other alliances.

I would give top priority here to the construction of a political and strategic alliance between Paris, Berlin, and Moscow, extending it, if possible, to Peking and Delhi. I expressly say political, with the objective of restoring international pluralism and the UN to all their proper functions, and strategic, with the objective of constructing together the military forces capable of meeting the American challenge. These three or four powers have all the requisite technological and financial means, strengthened by their traditional military capabilities, to construct such forces, before which the United States would appear much weaker. The American challenge and its criminal ambitions force this response. These ambitions are excessive and it is necessary to prove it. Forming an anti-hegemonist front is today the very first priority, just as forming an anti-Nazi alliance was yesterday.

This strategy would reconcile the "pro-Europeans" of groups two, three, and four with the "non-Europeans" of the left. It would create favorable conditions for the resumption later of a European project, probably even integrating a Great Britain freed from its submission to the United States and an Eastern Europe rid of its servile culture. We must be patient, as this will take much time.

There are some serious obstacles to overcome in order for this strategy to make progress, however.

First obstacle: the liberal virus, from which the group symbolized by the French, German, and Russian governments must be freed. It is possible for them to give their national political economies an acceptable social content. France and Germany can compel the European Union to accept it. Existing agreements permit it. Besides, the firm decision of these two countries to make it happen would reverse the relations of forces in many other countries in their favor.

Second obstacle: the Euro. The existence of this unique currency, without even an embryonic common state, is undesirable, because in present conditions every advance in this direction would strengthen the pro-American camp. It constitutes a large part of the challenge defined in the first obstacle above because the management of the Euro is both collective and liberal. Fortunately, Great Britain does not participate in that management. France and Germany can, together, turn the management of the Euro in a different direction. A project inspired by the Tobin tax would allow this to happen simultaneously with liberation from the financial tribute that is indispensable to the implementation of the aggressive strategy of the United States.

Third obstacle: the project of a "European constitution" (which Giscard d'Estaing supports). It is necessary to reject that project because, quite simply, the conditions do not exist for a (supranational) European political power to be, in the immediate future, anything other than a projection of the power of the United States. Far from strengthening the autonomy of Europe, all immediate progress towards a European political structure would reinforce Washington's control over its subordinate allies. It is necessary to postpone possible European progress towards such a structure to a more distant phase, when social and political forces and their ideological expressions will be sufficiently advanced to permit it.

Fourth obstacle, which recapitulates all of them: the Americanization of thought which carries within itself the liberal virus that it is necessary to eradicate. Without any doubt, this Americanization has progressed over the last half century. It degrades Europe, causes it to regress, forces it to abandon everything progressive in its contribution to the capitalist stage of human development, i.e., the antidotes which allowed it to resist the liberal virus and promote democracy in spite of it. (I expressly say stage—that is to say, a way-station which must be conceived as such, not as "the end of history".)

"Old Europe" has nothing to learn from "young America". There will be no progress possible on any European project as long as the American strategy is not foiled.

2. SECOND CHALLENGE: REESTABLISH THE SOLIDARITY OF THE PEOPLES OF THE SOUTH

Guidelines for a grand alliance on the basis of which the peoples and states of the South could reconstruct their solidarity.

Both from the positions taken by certain States of the South and the ideas that guide them, one can see guidelines taking shape for a possible renewal of a "front of the South". These positions concern the political domain as much as the economic management of globalization.

(a)

On the political plane: condemnation of the new principle of the United States' policy ("preventive war") and demand for the evacuation of all foreign military bases in Asia, Africa and Latin America.

Since 1990, Washington's uninterrupted military interventions have focused on the Arab Middle East, including Iraq and Palestine (for the latter, via the unconditional support for Israel), the Balkans (Yugoslavia, new implantations of the United States in Hungary, Rumania and Bulgaria), Central Asia, and the Caucasus (Afghanistan, Central Asia and the former Soviet Caucasus).

The objectives pursued by Washington include several parts:

1. The seizure of the most important petroleum regions of the world and consequently the exertion of pressure on Europe and Japan with the aim of subjecting them to the status of subordinate allies;
2. The establishment of permanent American military bases in the heart of the Old World (Central Asia is equally distant from Paris, Johannesburg, Moscow, Peking, Singapore);
3. Consequently the preparation of other "preventive wars" to come, above all aiming at large countries which are likely to assert themselves as partners with which "it is necessary to negotiate" (in the first place China, but equally Russia and India).

The realization of this objective implies the installation of puppet regimes imposed by the armed forces of the United States in the countries of the region in question. From Peking to Delhi and Moscow it is understood more and more that the wars "made in USA" definitely form a menace directed more against China, Russia, and India than against their immediate victims, such as Iraq.

To return to the Bandung position—demanding no American military bases in Asia and Africa—is from now on the order of the day, even if, in the circumstances of the moment, the non-aligned countries have agreed to be silent on the question of the American protectorates in the Persian Gulf.

The nonaligned countries have here taken positions close to those that France and Germany defended in the Security Council, thus accentuating the diplomatic and moral isolation of the aggressor. In turn, the Franco–African summit has helped the possible alliance which is taking shape between Europe and the South. This summit was not just one of "French Africa" because the continent's Anglophone States were present as well.

(b)

In the domain of the economic management of the world system, the guidelines for an alternative that the South could collectively defend are equally taking shape, because here the interests of all countries in the South are convergent.

1. The idea that the international transfers of capital should be controlled has returned. In fact, the opening of capital accounts, imposed by the IMF as an additional dogma of "liberalism", seeks only one objective: to facilitate the massive transfer of capital to the United States in order to cover the growing American deficit—itself the result both of deficiencies in the economy of the United States and implementation of its strategy for military control of the planet.

   The countries of the South have no interest in facilitating the loss of their capital and the possible devastations caused by speculative raids. Consequently, being subjected to all the hazards of "flexible exchange", which proceeds as a logical deduction from the opening capital accounts, should be called into question. Instead, instituting systems of regional organizations which would assure a relative stability in exchange rates deserves to be the object of systematic research and debate among the nonaligned countries and the Group of 77. After all, in the Asian financial crisis of 1997, Malaysia took the initiative to reestablish control over exchanges and it won the battle. The IMF itself was compelled to admit it.

2. The idea of regulating foreign investment has returned. Undoubtedly, the countries of the Third World do not envisage shutting the door to all foreign investment, as was the case with some of them in the past. On the contrary, direct investments are solicited. But the methods of welcoming this investment are once again the object of critical reflection. Certain milieux in Third World governments are aware of these reflections. Closely related

to the regulation of foreign investment is the contestation of the notion of intellectual and industrial property rights which the WTO wishes to impose on the Third World. It is understood that this notion, far from favoring "transparent" competition in open market, would, on the contrary, strengthen transnational monopolies.

3. Many among the countries of the South realize once again that they cannot dispense with a national agricultural policy that takes into account both protecting the peasantry from the devastating consequences of their accelerated disintegration under the effect of the "new competition" promoted by the WTO and preserving the security of national food supplies.

In reality, the opening of the markets for agricultural products, which allows the United States, Europe and some rare countries from the South (those of the cone of South America) to export their surplus to the Third World, consequently threatens the objective of securing the national food supply. There is nothing to counterbalance that effect, because the products of the Third World peasantry encounter insurmountable difficulties in the markets of the North. This liberal strategy, which disintegrates the peasantry and intensifies the migration from the country to urban shantytowns, encourages the reappearance of peasant struggles in the South, which, in turn, alarms the authorities.

The agricultural question is often discussed, particularly in the arena of the WTO, under the exclusive angle of subsidies granted by Europe and the United States not only to products from their farmers, but equally to their agricultural exports. This fixation on the sole question of world commerce in agricultural products clearly indicates a refusal to take into account the major preoccupations invoked above. In addition, it entails curious ambiguities, when the countries of the global South are invited to defend positions even more liberal than those adopted in reality by governments of the North, to the applause of the World Bank. (But since when has the World Bank defended the interests of the South against the North?) Nothing prevents the governments of the North from separating the subsidies granted to their farmers from those intended to support the dumping of the North's agricultural exports (after all if we defend the principle of income redistribution in our countries, then the countries of the North equally have this right!). It would be much better if the countries of the South were to orient their agricultural development towards the satisfaction of the needs of their internal markets—which are immense and should have priority—freeing themselves as much as possible from the vicissitudes of the world market for food products. It will come little by little.

4. The debt is no longer only felt as financially insupportable. Its legitimacy is beginning to be called into question. A demand is taking shape which has as its objective the unilateral repudiation of odious and illegitimate debts and includes the initial formulation of an international law for debt—worthy of the name—which still does not exist.

A generalized audit of debts would, in fact, make it evident that a significant proportion of the debts are illegitimate, odious and sometimes even vicious. The interest alone paid on the debt has reached a volume such that the juridically-based but unreasonable demand for its repayment would in reality cancel out the current debt and cause the entire operation to appear as a downright primitive form of pillage.

In order for the challenge to the debt's legitimacy to succeed, the idea that foreign debts should be regulated by normal and civilized legislation, just like domestic debts, should be part of a campaign launched within the context of supporting the development of international law and reinforcing its legitimacy. It is well known that it is precisely because law is silent in this area that the question is regulated only by brutal and uncivilized relations of force. These relations thus allow international debts to be accepted as legitimate which, if they were domestic, (the creditor and debtor belonging to the same nation and answerable to its judicial system) would lead debtor and creditor in front of the courts for "criminal conspiracy".

3. THIRD CHALLENGE: RECONSTRUCT A PEOPLES' INTERNATIONALISM

New International Perspectives

In order to be able to envisage a "remake" of Bandung, it is necessary to recognize that the world system today is very different in its fundamental structures from the one that existed at the end of the Second World War.

At that time the nonaligned countries were situated in a militarily bipolar world which prevented the imperialist countries from brutally intervening in their affairs. In addition, this bipolarity joined the partners of the capitalist centers—the United States, Western Europe, and Japan—into a unified camp. Thus the political and economic conflict for liberation and development opposed Asia and Africa to a unified imperialist camp. The concepts of autocentered development and of delinking and the strategies inspired by them responded to this challenge in those conditions.

Today, the world is militarily unipolar. Simultaneously, fractures seem to be appearing between the United States and certain European countries concerning the political management of a globalized system that is henceforth entirely aligned with the principles of liberalism, in principle at least. Are these fractures conjunctural and of limited import or do they indicate lasting changes? Proposals for a strategy to face these new conditions are based on hypotheses which should be made explicit, in order to facilitate the discussion of their possible validity.

FIRST HYPOTHESIS: *From now on, imperialism is a collective imperialism (of the Triad)*

Over the course of the preceding phases of the development of capitalist globalization, there was always more than one center. These centers were held together by relations of permanently violent competition to the point that the conflict among imperialisms occupied a central place on the historical scene. The return of globalized liberalism beginning in 1980 compels us to rethink the structure of the center in the contemporary system. At least on the plane of the management of liberal economic globalization, the states of the central Triad apparently form of a solid bloc.

The unavoidable question then is this: do the changes in question denote a lasting qualitative change—the center is no longer plural but is becoming decidedly "collective"—or are they only conjunctural?

One could attribute this evolution to transformations in the conditions of competition.

Only a few decades ago, giant companies would engage in their battles of competition essentially in national markets, whether that of the United States (the largest national market in the world) or even those of the European states (despite their modest size in relation to the United States, which is a disadvantage for them). The victors in each national market could put themselves in a good position in the world market. Today the size of the market necessary to win the first set of matches approaches 500–600 million potential consumers. Thus, the battle must be engaged directly on the world market and won on this terrain. The winners are those who prevail, then, in this essential market and, in addition, in their respective national terrains. Expanded globalization becomes the principal framework for the activity of the large firms. In other words, in the relationship between national and global, the conditions of causality are reversed: formerly, national power controlled a world presence, today the reverse is true. As a result, transnational firms, regardless of their nationality, have common interests in the management of the world market. These interests are superimposed on the permanent commercial conflicts that define all forms of competition peculiar to capitalism, whatever they may be.

SECOND HYPOTHESIS: *In the system of collective imperialism, the United States does not command decisive economic advantages.*

Current opinion is that the military power of the United States forms only the tip of the iceberg, extending the superiority of this country into all domains, notably economic, but even political and cultural. Submitting to the hegemonism it aspires to is thus unavoidable.

In fact, the productive system of the United States is far from being "the most efficient in the world". On the contrary, almost none of its segments would be certain to prevail over its competitors in a truly open market as liberal economists conceive of it. Witness the commercial deficit of the United States which has grown worse year after year, moving from $100 billion in 1989 to $450 billion in 2000. In addition, this deficit concerns practically every segment of the productive system. Even the surplus from which the United States benefited in the area of high technology goods, which was $35 billion in 1990, has henceforth given way to a deficit. The competition between Ariane and the rockets of NASA, and between Airbus and Boeing, are evidence of the vulnerability of the American advantage. Faced with the high technology products of Europe and Japan, with the common manufactured products of China, South Korea, and the other industrialized countries of Asia and Latin America, and the agricultural products of Europe and the cone of South America, the United States would probably not prevail without recourse to the "extra economic" means which violate the rules of liberalism forced on its competitors!

In fact, the United States benefits from fixed comparative advantages only in the armaments sector, precisely because this sector largely escapes the rules of the market and benefits from the support of the state. Undoubtedly, this advantage involves some fallout for the civilian sector (the Internet is the most well-known example of this), but it is equally the origin of severe distortions which create handicaps for many productive sectors.

The North American economy lives as a parasite to the detriment of its partners in the world system. As Emmanuel Todd points out, "the United States depends for 10 per cent of its industrial consumption on imported goods not covered by the export of its national products". The world produces, the United States (whose national savings are practically nil) consumes. The "advantage" of the United States is that of a predator whose deficit is covered by the contributions of others, either by consent or by force. The means implemented by Washington to compensate for its deficiencies are diverse: repeated unilateral violations of the principles of liberalism, armaments exports, the pursuit of super-profits from petroleum (which supposes the systematic exploitation of the producers, the real motive behind the wars in central Asia and Iraq). The fact remains that the main part of the American deficit is covered by contributions of capital from Europe,

Japan, and the South (the rich petroleum countries and the comprador classes of every Third World country, including the poorest), to which is added a regular draining of resources in the guise of servicing the debt, imposed on almost all countries in the periphery of the world system.

The solidarity of the dominant segments of transnationalized capital in all the partners of the Triad is real and is expressed in their rallying to globalized neoliberalism. The United States is seen in this perspective as the defender of these common interests—of necessary, by military means. The fact remains that Washington does not intend to share equally the profits from its leadership. On the contrary, the United States aims to make vassals of its allies, and in this spirit is only ready to grant minor concessions to the subaltern allies of the Triad. Will this conflict of interests within dominant capital lead to a rupture in the Atlantic alliance? This is not impossible, but it is not probable.

THIRD HYPOTHESIS: *The project of military control of the planet is intended to compensate for the deficiencies in the economy of the United States. This project threatens everyone in the Third World.*

This hypothesis follows logically from the preceding one. Washington's strategic decision to profit from their overwhelming military superiority and, in this perspective, to resort to "preventive wars" decided and planned by it alone aims at ruining any hope of a "great nation" (such as China, India, Russia, Brazil) or a regional coalition in the Third World from becoming an actual partner in shaping the world system, even if it be a capitalist one.

FOURTH HYPOTHESIS: *The South should and can liberate itself from liberal illusions and undertake the construction of renewed forms of autocentered development.*

For the moment, undoubtedly, the governments of the South still seem to be fighting for a "true neoliberalism" in which the partners from the North, as well as those from the South, would agree to "play the game". The countries of the South will find that this hope is illusory.

Thus, it will be necessary for them to return to the unavoidable concept that all development is autocentered. To develop is first of all to define national objectives that would allow for both the modernization of productive systems and the creation of internal conditions in which those systems would begin to serve social progress. Then the forms of the relations of the nation in question to the developed capitalist centers would be subjected to the requirements of this logic. This definition of delinking (mine)—which is not the same as autarky—places the concept of development at the opposite pole from (liberalism's) principle of "structural adjustment" to the demands of globalization, in which development is forcibly subjected to the exclusive imperatives of the expansion of dominant transnational capital, there by deepening inequality on the world scale.

FIFTH HYPOTHESIS: *The United States' option in favor of militarizing globalization strikes directly at the interests of Europe and Japan.*

This hypothesis follows from the second one. The objective of the United States, among other things, aims at placing its European and Japanese partners in a subordinate position (in a position of being vassals) by using military means to take over all the decisive resources of the planet (petroleum in particular). The American oil wars are anti-European wars. Europe (and Japan) can partially respond to this strategy by moving closer to Russia, which is capable, in part, of supplying them with petroleum and some other essential primary materials.

SIXTH HYPOTHESIS: *Europe should and can liberate itself from the liberal virus. However, this initiative cannot come from the segments of dominant capital, but must come from the people.*

The dominant segments of capital are of course defenders of globalized neoliberalism and as a result agree to pay the price of their subordination to the North American leader. So far, European governments believe they must give exclusive priority to defending the interests of these segments.

Peoples across Europe have a different vision both of the European project, which they want to be a social project, and of their relations with the rest of the world, which they want to see managed by law and justice. They have expressed this vision at the present time by condemning—by an overwhelming majority—the deviation of the United States. If this humanist and democratic political culture of "old Europe" prevails— and it is possible that it will—then an authentic rapprochement among Europe, Russia, China, Asia, and Africa would form the foundation upon which it would be possible to construct a democratic and peaceful pluricentric world.

The major contradiction between Europe and the United States does not lie between the interests of dominant capital from each place, but is found on the field of political culture. In Europe, a left alternative always remains possible. This alternative would simultaneously force a break with neoliberalism (and the abandonment of the vain hope of subjecting the United States to its requirements, thus allowing European capital to engage in economic competition on a terrain that has not been already undermined) and alignment with the political strategies of the United States. The surplus capital that Europe is so far satisfied to place in the United States could then be set aside for an economic and social revival, without which the latter would remain impossible. But from the moment that Europe chooses, by this means, to give priority to its economic and social progress, the spurious health of the economy of the United States would collapse and the American ruling class would be confronted with its own social problems. Such is the meaning that I give to my conclusion that "Europe will be left or it will not be".

In order to succeed, it is necessary for the Europeans to rid themselves of the illusion that the card of liberalism should be, and could be, played "honestly" by all and then all would go well. The United States cannot renounce its choice of an asymmetric practice of liberalism because that is the only means by which it can compensate for its own deficiencies.

European political cultures are diverse, even if to a certain extent they contrast with that of the United States. There are in Europe political, social, and ideological forces that support—often with lucidity—the vision of "another Europe" (social and friendly in its relations with the South). But there is also Great Britain which, since 1945, has made the historical choice of aligning itself unconditionally with the United States. There are the political cultures of the ruling classes of Eastern Europe, fashioned by a culture of servitude, which bowed down before Hitler, then Stalin, and today Bush. There are populisms of the right (nostalgic for Franco and Mussolini in Spain and Italy) which are "pro-American". Will the conflict among these cultures cause Europe to break apart? Will it definitively result in an alignment with Washington or in a victory for progressive humanist and democratic cultures?

SEVENTH HYPOTHESIS: *The reconstruction of a solid front of the South implies the participation of its peoples.*

The political regimes in place in many of the countries of the South are not democratic, which is the least that one can say, and sometimes they are frankly odious. These authoritarian structures of power favor the comprador fractions whose interests are linked to the expansion of global imperialist capital.

The alternative—the construction of a front of the peoples of the South—passes through democratization. This democratization will necessarily be difficult and long, but the way towards it surely does not lie in the installation of puppet governments which hand over the resources of their countries to be pillaged by North American transnationals. These regimes are even more fragile, less credible, and less legitimate than those they replace under the protection of the American invader. After all, the objective of the United States is not the promotion of democracy in the world despite its purely hypocritical discourses in this matter.

EIGHTH HYPOTHESIS: *A new internationalism of peoples associating Europeans, Asians, Africans, and Americans is therefore possible.*

This hypothesis, which follows from the preceding and

forms a conclusion to it, means that the conditions exist that would at least allow a rapprochement of all the peoples of the Old World. The rapprochement would be crystallized at the international diplomatic level by stabilizing the Paris–Berlin–Moscow–Peking axis, strengthened by the development of friendly relations between this axis and the reconstituted Afro-Asiatic front.

It goes without saying that advances in this direction would reduce to nothing the excessive and criminal ambitions of the United States. The latter would then be forced to accept coexistence with nations determined to defend their own interests.

At the present moment, this objective should be considered an absolute priority. The deployment of the American project overdetermines the stake of every struggle: no social and democratic advance will be lasting as long as the American plan has not been foiled.

NINTH HYPOTHESIS: *Questions relative to cultural diversity should be discussed within the context of the new international perspectives outlined here.*

Cultural diversity is a fact. But it is a complex and ambiguous fact. Diversities inherited from the past, as legitimate as they may be, are not necessarily synonymous with diversity in the construction of the future. It is not only necessary to admit this, but to investigate it.

To call upon only the diversities inherited from the past (political Islam, Hindutva, Confucianism, Negritude, chauvinist ethnicities, and more) is frequently a demagogic exercise of autocratic and comprador powers, which enables them both to evade the challenge represented by the universalization of civilization and to submit in fact to the dictates of dominant transnational capital. In addition, the exclusive insistence on these heritages divides the Third World, by opposing political Islam and Hindutva in Asia, Muslims, Christians, and practitioners of other religions in Africa. Basing a united political front of the South on new principles is the means of overcoming these divisions maintained by American imperialism. But then what are and can be the universal "values" upon which the future can be built? The Western-centered and restrictive interpretation of these values legitimizes unequal development, an inherent product of globalized capitalist expansion yesterday and today. It must be rejected. But then how to promote genuinely universal concepts, with contributions from everyone? It is time for this debate to begin.

Works Referred to in the Text

Achcar, Gilbert. *The Clash of Barbarisms: September 11 and the Making of the New World Disorder.* New York: Monthly Review Press, 2002.

Blum, William. *Rogue State: A Guide to the World's Only Superpower.* Monroe, ME: Common Courage Press, 2000.

Braudel, Fernand. *Civilization and Capitalism, 15th–18th Century.* Berkeley: University of California Press, 1992.

Castells, Manuel. *The Rise of the Network Society.* Câmbridge, MA: Blackwell, 1996.

Fukuyama, Francis. *The End of History and the Last Man.* New York: Free Press, 1992.

Hardt, Michael And Antonio Negri. *Empire.* Cambridge, MA: Harvard University Press, 2000.

Huntington, Samuel. *The Clash of Civilizations and the Remaking of World Order.* New York: Simon & Schuster, 1996.

Kautsky, Karl. *The Agrarian Question.* London: Zwan Publications, 1988.

Rawls, John. *A Theory of justice.* Combridge, MA: Belknap Press of Harvard University Press, 1999.

Rifkin, Jeremy. *The End of Work: The Decline of the Global Labor Force and the Dawn of the Post-Market Era.* New York: G.P. Putnam's Sons, 1995.

Todd, Emmanuel. *Aprés l'Empire,* Paris: Gallimard, 2002.

Touraine, Alain. *Critique of Modernity.* Cambridge, MA: Blackwell, 1995.

Wallerstein, Immanuel. *The Modern World-System: Capitalist Agriculture and the Origins of the European World-Economy in the Sixteenth Century.*

New York: Academic Press, 1976.

Works by the Author

BOOKS

Amin, Samir. *Eurocentrism.* New York: Monthly Review Press, 1989.

Amin, Samir and François Houtart, Eds. *Mondialisations des résistances, l'état des luttes 2002.* Paris: L'Harmattan, 2002.

Amin, Samir. *Obsolescent Capitalism: Contemporary Politics and Global Disorder.* London: Zed Press, 2004.

Amin, Samir. *Specters of Capitalism: A Critique of Current Intellectual Fashions.* New York: Monthly Review Press, 1998.

ARTICLES

Amin, Samir. "Confronting the Empire", *Al-Ahram Weekly,* no. 627 (February 27–March 5, 2003).

Amin, Samir. "Judaïsme, Christianisme, Islam: Réflexion sur leurs spécificités réelles ou prétendus", *Social Compass,* vol,. 46, no. 4 (1999).

Amin, Samir. "Mondialisation et démocratie, une contradiction majeure de notre époque", *Recherches Internationales,* no. 55 (1999).

Amin, Samir. "Quelles alternatives à la dimension destructive de l'accumulation du capital?" *Alternatives Sud,* vol. VIII, no. 2 (2001).

Amin, Samir. "Marx et la démocratie", *La Pensée*, no. 328 (2001).

Amin, Samir. "Mondialisation ou apartheid à l'échelle mondiale", *Actuel Marx*, no. 31 (2002).

Index

Printed and bound by CPI Group (UK) Ltd, Croydon, CR0 4YY

13/04/2025

14656489-0003